Midlife and Older Women

Midlife and Older Women

Family Life, Work and Health in Jamaica

Joan Rawlins

University of the West Indies Press
Jamaica • Barbados • Trinidad and Tobago

University of the West Indies Press
1A Aqueduct Flats   Mona
Kingston 7   Jamaica
www.uwipress.com

10 09 08 07 06   5 4 3 2 1

CATALOGUING IN PUBLICATION DATA

Rawlins, Joan M.
Midlife and older women: family life work and health in Jamaica / Joan Rawlins.
p. cm.
Based on the author's PhD thesis — Institute of Social Studies, The Hague, 1996.
Includes bibliographical references.
ISBN: 976-640-183-7

1. Middle-aged women – Jamaica. 2. Older women – Jamaica. 3. Women – Employment
– Jamaica. 5. Women – Health and hygiene – Jamaica. I. Title.

HQ1059.5.J3R385 2006   331.4'097292

Book and cover design by Robert Kwak.

Printed in the United States of America.

CONTENTS

ILLUSTRATIONS

TABLES

ACKNOWLEDGEMENTS

So impressed have I been with the work of women in midlife and older, as I have observed them in Jamaican society, that I wanted to do something to ensure that a wider audience would be given an opportunity to contemplate the lives of this group of women. These women do yeoman service for their families and, by extension, the Jamaican society and they deserve to have some part of their stories recorded for posterity. This book owes its heart to these women, to whom I am very grateful.

To the Institute of Social Studies in The Hague and the Government of the Netherlands I wish to say thanks, for funding the PhD scholarship and dissertation from which this book arises. I am grateful for the advice and guidance I received from supervisors Dr Renee Pittin, Professor Geertje Lycklama and Dr Ines Smyth, which continued to be especially valuable to me as I worked on this book. I am also indebted to others, including Professor Maureen Cain, formerly of the University of the West Indies, Trinidad and Tobago, and to Dr Patricia Mohammed and Professor Rhoda Reddock of the Centre for Gender and Development Studies, the University of the West Indies, Trinidad and Tobago, who encouraged me as I sought to make the transition from dissertation to book. Thanks also to Professor Joyce Toney, Head of the Women's Studies Department, Hunter College, New York, who facilitated me by affording me space at Hunter College for a short period in 2003, allowing me to work undisturbed on this book.

To my friends and colleagues who encouraged me along the way I give thanks. This list is not exhaustive, but special thanks are due to Roanna Gopaul, Stephanie Pile, Jessica Byron, Eudine Barriteau, Michelle Rowley, Monica Gordon and Paula Ellis.

To the Centre for Gender and Development Studies, University of the West Indies, Mona, for facilitating my fellowship in The Hague, what now seems like so many years ago, thanks. Thanks also to the University of the West Indies, St Augustine, for affording me academic leave early in 2003 to spend time with this book project.

To Dr Pamela Collins, thanks for helpful editorial suggestions and guidelines as I sought to bring closure to this project. I am deeply indebted to her professionalism.

Thanks also to my siblings, Donnet De Freitas, Lorna Joseph and Carl Porteous, and to my children, Samantha, Sekou and Carey Rawlins, who were all sources of encouragement. Last, but definitely not least, thanks to my husband Sam, who has been a tremendous source of inspiration and encouragement for every bit of writing that I have ever chosen to do.

INTRODUCTION

A great gulf exists between what is known and what should be known about women in midlife and older, in order to understand their lives. In Jamaica, women over fifty years old are taken for granted, although demographically and socially they have been, and continue to be, a force to be reckoned with in the society. They are such a force because of their positive contributions to family, community and the economy. They often run their households and take responsibility for the care of elderly parents, elderly or sick siblings, ailing spouses and other members of the community. They may mind children from the community as well as their own grandchildren, freeing younger women to participate more fully in the labour force. They are active in their communities, organizing as leaders and participants. They are diligent and resourceful in the work that they do. They travel abroad on economic missions as "informal commercial importers", they are higglers (vendors) in the marketplace, they run shops or they work from home as seamstresses or domestics. Those fortunate enough to have higher education often continue, even after retirement, to provide their professional services for the benefit of others. This group of women is forceful and energetic; they are to be found everywhere, active and participating in the life of society.

However, despite all that they do, the roles of midlife and older women are often taken for granted by those around them, and even by themselves. There is still a sense that the role of these women in society is not recognized. For example, in 1990–91, when the research for this study was being done, one never heard folk songs or popular songs that sang the praises of these women, nor was there much documentation about their lives. The following statement from the Jamaica Bureau of Women's Affairs (1982, 2) adequately summarized some of the concerns which, as a researcher, I had at the time: "Despite the testimony of history, tradition, culture and statistics to the crucial role women play in Jamaican society, women's activities in the family and the workplace remain undervalued and under-supported." The Bureau's reference was not specific to older women, but the point is made that if all women were under-valued, with the cultural practice of overlooking older women, they would have been doubly overlooked.

This study is essentially one about the family life, work and health of so-called midlife and older women in Jamaica in the early 1990s. Here reference is being made to two groups of women who are usually kept separate in demographic studies. At the point of data collection and in the data analysis these women are recognizable as being in "midlife" (fifty to fifty-nine years old) and "older" (sixty to seventy-four years old). We are able to speak about them at times as such, while at other times it is convenient to refer to them as "older women". This age group was targeted because the intention was to focus on women who were no longer involved in their child-bearing years.

This book argues that, while the familial contribution of older women is sometimes acknowledged by the society, outside of academic discourse they tended, up to 1991, to have been seen as "carers" rather than "minders" (Rodman 1978). Even in the negative presentation of their sexuality, older women are portrayed as caregivers.[1]

The paucity of research on this age group in the 1980s and early 1990s was not unique, and middle-aged and older women were frequently overlooked. Sennott-Miller (1989, 1) makes the point that "little is known about women at midlife and older in the Caribbean". In Jamaica for that period, the few in-depth studies that had been done on older women (Eldemire 1989, 1993; Grell 1987) were carried out in relation to women's health, and had concentrated on women over sixty years old, including some very old women.

Within the broader area of the Caribbean, over the past fifty years, numerous studies of Caribbean families have been done: Simey 1946; Henriques 1953; R.T. Smith 1956; Clarke 1957; M.G. Smith 1962; Dirks and Kerns 1976; Roberts and Sinclair 1978; Whitehead 1978; and Rodman 1978, to name only a few. Many of these researchers, especially those who wrote prior to the 1970s, were concerned with what they saw as the disorganization of the family, with the so-called social pathology of the family and the marginality of the Caribbean male. In spite of the wealth of information that these and other studies incorporated, they tended to exclude both the problems of older persons in the society and their contributions. A particular area of neglect was the older woman and her contribution. Some of these studies informed us on a wide range of issues: for example, studies by Massiah (1982) and Powell (1984) had as their target group women who had not passed beyond the years of childbearing and child rearing; clearly these researchers were fascinated by these younger women and their lives, prior to the late 1980s. This is understandable as, in terms of straight demographics, there are usually more of that age group of women than there are women fifty to seventy-four years old. In 1990, the female population of Jamaica aged twenty to forty-four years was 442,800, while the female population fifty years and over was 195,000 (Planning Institute of Jamaica 1990). These younger women also tended to have children still in need of care, and husbands and partners whose relationships with them have encouraged so much research-attention in the past. In the intervening years since the research for this book was done, research on Caribbean women and their families has continued. Notable among these studies has been the work of Momsen (1993), Mohammed and Perkins (1999) and Rawlins (2002a).

Some of the important questions to which answers were sought when the research began were: What is the nature of the family life of women in their post-child-bearing years? What is the nature of their economic life as it relates to work, pensions, remittances and housing? What is the nature of their other relationships, for example, those in the public sphere, when they interact with health and other governmental agencies and the community? All of these relationships appeared to be governed by similar discourses about the mature woman (discourses being, for my purposes, what it is possible to speak of at a given moment). Discourses are "the structured ways of knowing, which are produced in, and are the shapers of, culture" (Ramazanoglu 1993, 23). Thus, discourses are produced by the culture but are also part of what makes the culture what it is.

To answer the questions that were posed and to analyse the relationships in which the women lived, a number of theories and concepts were explored, including concepts of power and class. The concept "power" was used to understand better the multifaceted relationships in which midlife and older women were involved on a daily basis.[2]

THEORETICAL UNDERPINNINGS OF THE RESEARCH

Midlife and older women in Jamaica are involved in complex relationships, whether these operate within the home with their spouses, sons, daughters, grandchildren and other relatives; within the community; or in relation to their involvement with the state and its various institutions. The concept "discursive power" as it has been expounded by Michel Foucault was used to make sense of the lives of those women and to map the correlations between the various spheres of their lives mentioned above.

Foucault's approach to power was especially useful to me because of the multifaceted ways in which he conceptualizes power. Unlike many theorists before him, Foucault does not present power as only repressive or structural, but as dynamic and subtle. He states: "Power is everywhere; not because it embraces everything, but because it comes from everywhere ... it is the name that one attributes to a complex strategical situation ..." (Foucault 1971, 93).

Foucault makes a connection between the body and power. He argues that the "disciplined" individual arrives at the point whereby "the body" controls itself, that is, it does what is required even without being told. That certainly was the situation that I discovered with many of the older Jamaican women I met. Foucault speaks of such bodies, disciplined bodies, as "docile bodies" – bodies that are useful and programmed, so to speak, to do what society requires of them. Foucault also makes reference to "discourse" as a source of power, and to resistance, to no single truth, to counter-discourses, repressed discourses and ambivalent discourses.

While Foucault's explication of power was in part useful in understanding power in the lives of the women who were the focus of this study, it did not sufficiently allow for the analysis of power in every situation in their lives. I therefore need to acknowledge that other factors, such as class, patriarchy, ageism, women's multiple identities and the sexual division of labour were also important in determining the power relations in the lives of these midlife and older women.

Additionally, the research that this book embodies sought to understand these older women's acceptance of certain values in the society, which in operation, might be seen to burden their existence.

Work

As we sought, through the literature, to understand the nature of the power relations in which older women in Jamaica live and organize their lives, it was inevitable that the issue of work, paid and unpaid, would arise. Throughout their life cycle the majority of Jamaican women are faced with a double burden: they work outside the home and within the home. As they grow older, some might look forward to a lessening of their responsibilities, but many find themselves trapped in the physical support of grandchildren and ageing relatives, as well as continued employment in paid labour or self-employment.

Those women involved in the care of elderly relatives suffer a great deal in their social life, and economically, as they are sometimes forced to relinquish jobs and take on others more conducive to the caring lifestyle. Because some of them need to devote so much of their time and energy to these activities, the isolation that they suffer is burdensome. In this regard, Farkas and Himes (1997) show how older women's social activities are negatively impacted by their caregiving roles, while Rawlins (2001) notes that older women as caregivers reported that their caregiving had negatively impacted their health.

The questions that had to be asked in the context of Jamaica were these: Why should those women, especially the younger group, participate in any of this unpaid domestic work when there might still be a place for them within the established labour force? Why should they miss out on opportunities to become involved in employment, which might not only be financially more rewarding, but might present greater challenges and so provide them with a greater sense of achievement than they might obtain from continuing in caring roles within the home? Additionally, in the Jamaican context, we needed to know if the varied responses of older women to the needs of their family led to changes in the social relations between themselves and their family members. Other concerns, specifically related to waged work and familial power relations, were: What control did women have over their time and labour, and who determined whether or not they continued to work for an income?

The majority of Jamaican women, especially working-class women, who less frequently have the support of a spouse,[3] work very hard for their families and communities, in rural as well as urban areas, and their task is often a thankless one. Women do various jobs, from manual and unskilled jobs in the informal sector to jobs in the professions, such as engineering, law, medicine and the media. Jamaican women who are employed outside the home, whatever their class, will invariably have responsibilities within the home, before they leave home for work, and on their return home.

The lot of older Jamaican women, especially the working-class women, might be hard, but this research experience convinced me that the women about whom this book is written obtained a great deal of satisfaction from the contribution they made; and that in some situations they felt that they were accorded special respect, while at other times they received less respect than they had anticipated. Respect for older rural women has been demonstrated in the work of Durant-Gonzalez (1980) for Jamaica, where she showed that older women who were higglers had special respect in their communities. One of the issues this research sought to understand was: What is the comparable situation for urban women – are they in a position to claim the kind of respect that Durant-Gonzalez suggested for rural women?

Economic Situation

Prior to data collection and analysis the research assumption was that the life situation of the women of this age group would vary considerably according to differences in class, and that the lives of the women of the middle classes, especially the middle and upper middle class appeared to be less stressful and more predictable and ordered than the lives of lower-middle- and working-class women. We reasoned that economically, working-class women, and some women of the lower middle class, would be less secure during this period, as neither they nor their male partners would have been able to make the type of financial investments that well-established middle-class persons make and which are used to protect them against periods of non-employment and after retirement.

This was not meant to suggest that working-class women do not also attempt to plan for their future, but given the economic climate of Jamaica in 1990–91, realization of significant savings would have been difficult for such women. Two factors that would have contributed to these women's economic difficulties may be suggested. First, it might be shown that power relations as demonstrated through the sexual division of labour ensure that women are restricted to certain roles within the society. This division of labour operates even against older women, thus showing the pervasiveness of this division and its impact on the latter stages of the life cycle. Second, during the fifteen years or so prior to the research period, the cost of living had risen significantly in Jamaica; first during the socialist experiment of the government of the People's National Party during the period between 1972 and 1980, when parts of the bauxite industry were nationalized and bauxite production, a major income earner for the economy, was reduced. The country's difficulties were further exacerbated by the massive increase of oil prices on the world market. The cost of living rose even more during the free enterprise system of government of the Jamaica Labour Party, 1980 to 1989, with inflation and high levels of unemployment being experienced by the country. These difficulties continued into 1990: in that year, between June and December, the Jamaican dollar was devalued from J\$8 to US\$1 and J\$21 to US\$1. Because the Jamaican dollar is pegged to the US dollar and because of the high import content of goods consumed in Jamaica, the people of Jamaica experienced inflation that by early 1991 was said to be 60 per cent.

The Demographic and Social Situation

Given that the concern of this study was women aged fifty to seventy-four years, it is useful to situate the women in their place within the population. Jamaica, like many other countries, is experiencing a shift in the demographic structure of the population. The demographic data for Jamaica show that the population over sixty years of age has been increasing steadily since 1970, from 8.4 per cent of the total population in that year to 10.8 per cent in 1982 (Department of Statistics 1982, vii). The population fifty years and over increased from 343,170 in 1982 to 379,810 in 1990, with the majority (195,020 or 51.4 per cent) being women (Planning Institute of Jamaica 1990).[4]

This period from midlife on is a time of many changes for women; it is the period when women are most likely to become widowed, given the greater life expectancy of women over men. In Jamaica the average age of widowhood for women is sixty-one years; women are far more likely to be widowed and less likely to remarry than are men (Rawlins 1989a). Phillipson (1980, 187) notes that it is women rather than men who face the major agony of seeing a lifelong partner sicken and eventually die, and it is the women, often with scant community support, who have to reconstruct their lives in the aftermath of their partner's death.

For some, widowhood might be a heart-rending experience, especially if the relationship with the spouse or partner had been particularly satisfying. For others, widowhood might be the break they had been awaiting. This might also be the case where the husband had been ill for a long period, where the husband's illness had been extremely costly to the wife in terms of time and money, or where the relationship had not been a satisfying one. In these cases, the demise of the husband might present the wife with some relief from what she might have come to think of as a desperate situation.

The general literature on the subject of the financial situation of widows shows that the death of a spouse leads to a serious decline in economic well-being for the surviving member (Hyman 1983; Morgan 1981; Zick and Smith 1986). Research (Rawlins 1989b; Sanchez 1989) in Jamaica and Puerto Rico also suggests that the death of a male partner leads to economic difficulties for the female survivor. More recent international research (Wells and Kendig 1997; Carr et al. 2001) suggests that life after widowhood can be unpredictable.

In addition to economic problems, some Jamaican widows experience isolation when their children migrate and their grandchildren live abroad (Rawlins 1989a). Their strategies for coping during this dramatic life event, whether through their own resilience or through informal social support, are explored in the literature. The situation of unmarried women who have lost their partner is also considered.[5] It appears that women who have not married by the time they are in their fifties eventually separate from their common-law partners and continue to have their children and grandchildren live with them. Also at this time religion plays a very important role in the lives of older women, and their relationship with the church forces them to restrict themselves from relationships with men that would not win the approval of the church. It would seem that those women gain genuine satisfaction from their relationship with the church in ways that they had not done in earlier years and so might choose to spend their spare time in church activities rather than in activities with men.

In the literature on the Caribbean much is written about grandmother families. These are the families in which the grandmothers are the heads of the households and have in residence with them some of their own children, of varying ages, as well as their grandchildren. Much of this early literature (for example, Clarke 1957; Smith 1956) portrays the grandmother as only too anxious to take on the responsibility for her grandchildren. More recent research (Rawlins and Sargent 1989; Mohammed and Perkins 1999) suggests that grandmothers are far more reluctant and resistant to fulfilling their expected roles as grandmothers and providers than has been described for the stereotypical grandmother in earlier studies of Caribbean families.

Migration is a common experience for the people of Jamaica. The country has a long history of movements of people outward to the United States, Canada and Britain. Examples of some of these mass migrations would include those of the 1950s and 1960s to Britain, in which large numbers of men as well as women were involved. Earlier migrations involved mainly men who travelled off the island to work in Cuba, Panama and as farm workers in the United States. Other large-scale movements took place to destinations in the United States in the 1970s and 1980s. These population movements have resulted in the dispersal of Jamaican family members all over the world, and the outward movements have continued into the 1990s and 2000s, although at a much slower pace. It is as a result of this pattern of migration, and other outward population movements in the late 1970s during and after Jamaica's experiment with socialism and during structural adjustment, that some older women found that they had few close relatives on the island.

THE STUDY: PLANNING AND METHODOLOGY

The Objectives of the Research

The main objectives of the study from which this book arises were:

1. to analyse the concepts of family and household in Jamaica with particular reference to these women's domestic and extra-domestic responsibilities, opportunities, obligations and the power relations that operate within these contexts;

2. to analyse the realities of work in its various forms in particular relationship to the broader economic structures, the specificities of class and family, and the effects these interrelationships have on older women's work experience and opportunities;

3. to examine the formal and informal support structures available to women, relating this to the provision of social support within the family, the community and the nation as a whole and to the power relations in which such women exist;

4. to analyse the health situation of middle aged and older women and the power relations that come into play as they seek to ensure health care for themselves; and

5. to examine the issues relating to the intimate relations of their lives, taking into consideration the negativity in the discourses surrounding the sexuality of older women.

The Research Communities

Jamaica is a society of extremes, in which there are great disparities between the life situations of the rich and the poor. It is a very class-divided society, with 10 per cent of the population living in luxury while the poorest 10 per cent struggle each day to eke out a living. These disparities increased during the 1980s under the impact of structural adjustment programmes (Levitt 1991, 43) and, at the time of the study, all social levels of Jamaican society were feeling the effects of escalating inflation and reduced government spending. This research was, therefore, intended to address specificities of class, as well as age and family. Two communities were identified for study: one a traditional working-class community, August Town, and the other an established middle-class community, Hope Pastures. Working class here was determined by the type of housing, the occupation of most of the people and their general standard of education. Middle class was also determined on criteria established for housing, occupation and education.[6]

Although the two communities are separated by a distance of less than three miles, they are in effect worlds apart. What they have in common is that many of their members are employees of the University of the West Indies. These people, however, work in different job categories, as the communities comprise populations that differ considerably by class.

August Town

August Town is a community with the majority of its residents in the lower socio-economic bracket. It adjoins the more affluent neighbourhoods of Mona and the University of the West Indies community. It is easy to think of August Town as a "service community", because the workers of the community literally provide service to the University of the West Indies, the University Hospital and the residents of Mona, Mona Heights and Hope Pastures, which is the study-community located in proximity to the University of the West Indies.

FIGURE 1. Road going downhill in August Town

August Town in 1990–91 was an interesting and varied community, with a population of approximately eight thousand people. Unlike Hope Pastures, August Town is an older community with a colourful history.[7] It is a mixture of old and new, urban but not fully urban. The members of this community might be the owners of new or old cars, bicycles or motorcycles, new or old houses. In 1990–91 two or three members of this community were also proud owners of satellite dishes, which enabled them to receive the numerous TV channels available from the United States. And all this alongside the owners of goats and cattle, who could be seen taking their animals to pasture early in the morning or leading them home in the evenings.

Residents who had lived in August Town for more than thirty years spoke of the numerous changes that had taken place there over time. Perhaps the most striking change was

FIGURE 2. Woman awaiting transportation in August Town

the way in which the population had grown and the community had expanded, and the increase in the number of homes to accommodate this growth.

The community of August Town lies downhill from the University of the West Indies. The main road is the August Town Road, which is one mile long and proceeds as a gentle slope through the community.

FIGURE 3. Older woman in August Town

The main road has many houses on both sides: some large, some small, some are close to the roadway, while others are set back some distance from the road. Some of the houses are of concrete and reinforced steel and are sturdily constructed and in a good state of repair. Others are of wood, some also in a good state of repair, while others are less well constructed and in need of repair and a new coat of paint.

There are numerous small shops, rum bars, food stands, places of enterprise and churches along this road. The small food shops supply items that might be needed on a regular basis, such as sugar, rice, flour, bread, eggs, matches, salt and fruit juice. This road is the heart of the community. It could not be described as residential or commercial, but rather as an efficient mix of the two. It is a narrow road for the volume of traffic that it handles. There was perhaps a time when it was seen as a wide road, but that would have been when the population was smaller, when there were fewer cars always parked along the roadway, and when it was not a major bus route.

August Town, then as now, is a hive of activity. It bustles with vendors and with children

FIGURE 4. Improved shop and home in August Town

on their way to and from school, walking or attempting to board already overcrowded buses. Men can be seen standing outside the bars and the other shops; young, unemployed men, of whom there are many, stand ogling the young women as they pass. By day, August Town is a very busy community with people hustling, in many senses, in order to survive. By midday

FIGURE 5. Schoolchildren waiting for a bus in August Town

the pace is less frenetic and women can be seen making their way to the shops or in their yards washing, hanging out clothes, minding children or sweeping their yards. Middle-aged and older women can also be seen going about their business at all hours of the day, or in the yards doing chores similar to those being done by the younger women.

As dusk approaches, the activity heightens as workers returning home add to the multitude on the streets, mixing with the swelling numbers of young men and boys and smaller numbers of young women outside the shops in the semi-darkness of evening, listening to their portable radios and chatting and laughing. By evening the community takes on the semblance of a semi-rural community. Although it is not more than a mile from Mona and Mona Heights, two middle-income communities, not all the houses and shops in August Town receive electricity. This is not because the Jamaica Public Service Company does not provide the area with electricity, but because the financial situation of some of the community members does not allow them to receive this service.[8] Consequently, lighting is irregular and one comes upon a well-lit shop, then a well-lit house, and then an area of semi-darkness, which might be a yard with electricity but with poor illumination, or a yard using kerosene lamps. One gets a sense of rural life here because of the irregular lighting, but there is not much that is rural about August Town.

August Town has many facilities and was a fairly self-sufficient community until the early 1960s, when the demands of the population began to outgrow the resources of the community. It has residents who are homeowners and those who are employers of others within the community. Some of the homeowners occupy land that has been leased to them by the government. There are also numerous yard-type situations,[9] in which large numbers of people live in individual units, of one or two rooms, in larger houses within the yard. The owner of the yard often lives elsewhere, visiting the place periodically, most often to collect the rent.

August Town is the site of the University of the West Indies sewage treatment disposal plant and houses the incinerator where much of the garbage of the neighbouring middle-class communities is burnt. Some residents expressed their dissatisfaction with what they viewed as a potential danger to their community. Added to this is a mountain that rises from the lower levels of August Town, from which marl is quarried daily.[10] The marl digging was a massive commercial operation in 1990–91, which ensured that each day scores of uncovered trucks, heavily loaded with marl, passed through this community. The people of the community complained that the marl blew all over their houses, their furniture and their food. Some even complained that their asthma and other chest conditions had worsened since the marl digging operations began many years previously.

August Town has many positive features, but perhaps the most important advantage for its residents is its proximity to the University of the West Indies. Some argue that August Town has grown to its present population only because of its service functions to the university, which is perhaps the major employer of the adult population of August Town and its sister community Hermitage.

Many years ago, concerned individuals within the University of the West Indies Department of Social and Preventive Medicine became aware of the desperate health needs of the people of August Town and Hermitage. They felt that their needs were not being addressed despite the geographic proximity of the community to the University Hospital of the West Indies (UHWI), where medical specialists were available, and in a situation in which the medical personnel sometimes used the community as their research laboratory. The people of August Town spent most of their working hours serving the university community in numerous ways but were not benefiting from the available health resources. Consequently, a health centre and clinic was established, which sought to serve the needs of these low-income people.[11]

The health centre is viewed by many August Town residents somewhat as a community centre. Some members, men and women, often visit the centre, not because they are ill or to keep an appointment, but to make contact with community members and to be brought up to date with the goings-on of the community.

Hope Pastures

Hope Pastures is a community in Kingston, located about a mile from the University of the West Indies at Mona. Hope Pastures was established as a community in 1962. Before that time it was an area covered by trees, with very few houses. The Hope Pastures area was originally part of what was called the Hope Estate, which adjoins lands owned by the Ministry of Agriculture at Hope. The large complex includes the well-known Hope Botanical Gardens.

It was the development of a housing scheme there in 1962 that opened up the area, allowing it to become the residential

FIGURE 6. Impressive gate in Hope Pastures

area it is today. Some of the original owners confided to this researcher that they had had reservations about the houses, which had been built by the developers, as they had not been designed to individual specifications, but had been built ostensibly on a number of similar plans. These houses were first purchased by wealthy light-skinned or white Jamaicans,[12] and for some, the idea of having a house that had not been custom designed was almost ridiculous. Nevertheless, the houses were seen to be a bargain and the developers had no difficulty selling them.

Some of the original owners who were interviewed for this study were very pleased that they had purchased their houses when they did. In 1990, with the devaluation of the Jamaican dollar, the £6,000 that they had paid was equivalent to J$84,000, but those same houses were valued at J$900,000 and as much as J$1.5 million in 1991, for those that had been significantly improved.[13] In 1991, I did not meet one person who was disappointed or disgruntled at having bought a Hope Pastures house during the 1960s and 1970s. Instead a small number said that they regretted that they had not invested in a second house at the time.

Hope Pastures, from all appearances, was a pleasant, quiet neighbourhood. The houses were well designed and well kept, as were the yards and gardens. A number of the yards had signs that cautioned "Beware of bad dogs". All the yards were fenced; most had hedges and all had gates. The fences and hedges were well maintained in order to prevent the dogs from

FIGURE 7. Improved home in Hope Pastures

entering the streets and intruders from entering the yard. But, despite all these precautions, at the time of the survey, Hope Pastures had not been without its fair share of the types of problems that haunted some areas of Jamaican society. The people of the community had experienced many burglaries, by day as well as by night, and, in March 1991, a housewife was murdered as she tended her flowers in her garden. All the houses in Hope Pasture were equipped with burglar bars: high iron grills placed on the windows and doors. One respondent, who was especially cautious because she had had prowlers in her yard in the past, observed that during the day, when the community was

usually fairly quiet and had a deserted feeling, she never ventured into the yard without taking her dog with her.

By day, Hope Pastures was a very quiet place. Husbands and wives and young adults were away at work, and children and grandchildren were at school. Maids and gardeners were within the yards and homes doing their respective chores,

FIGURE 8. Home in lower Hope Pastures

sometimes unsupervised or under the supervision of housewives. By 4:00 P.M., Hope Pastures began to take on a new face: at this time children could be seen returning from school and the lively chatter of teenagers could be heard. There was an increase in traffic as parents returned from work, some having collected their children from school on the way home. Whereas earlier in the day one rarely met pedestrians on the road, all the traffic being vehicular, by late afternoon there were many pedestrians, mainly domestic helpers and gardeners walking home at the end of their workday. By about 7:30 P.M., the area changed once again into a much quieter community. There were lights on in the windows, and cars parked in the driveways and on the roads outside the houses. Also at that time of day many more men were to be seen in the community, parking their cars, and standing at their gates chatting to their neighbours or keeping an eye on the teenagers socializing outside. One had the feeling, from talking to residents, that, despite the security problems, Hope Pastures was a pleasant place to live.

Those residents of long standing with whom this researcher spoke all agreed that Hope Pastures had been a very fine place to live in earlier days. There had been a sense of community: the people knew one another and everyone was friendly. There was a Citizen's Association and parties were held at the local playing field. Some respondents reminisced about the house parties, the exchange of visits and the socializing that had been a common feature of life in Hope Pastures. The respondents of upper Hope Pastures stated that the community had not changed much since its establishment in 1963.[14] The houses were still owner-occupied and many of the original owners remained. Further down, in lower Hope Pastures, where most of the interviews were done, there

FIGURE 9. Improved home in lower Hope Pastures

appeared to have been many more changes. Some of the houses had changed owners three or four times and some were no longer owner-occupied. Generally, most of the houses in lower as well as upper Hope Pastures had been improved. The original houses had maid's quarters, but by 1990 most had an additional two bedrooms, as well as other rooms and facilities.

Data Sources

Data for the research project were obtained through a survey, case studies, the use of various libraries and library sources, and by discussions with specific people in the communities studied, as well as from interviews and discussions with other individuals in Kingston who were associated in one way or another with women in midlife. The main sources of data, however, were the survey and the case studies.[15]

The Women's Questionnaire

The objectives of the study included determination of how women coped in various areas of their life, given the framework of power that influences their daily experiences. The questionnaire had a total of 118 questions, the majority of which pursued the specific objectives of the research. Some of the questions were open-ended while others were structured. The questionnaire, though not explicitly subdivided, had implicit sections which sought to gain information on the following areas:

1. general demographic information;
2. education level;
3. family and power relationships;
4. issues related to closeness and control;
5. work and a wide range of economic concerns;
6. dependency;
7. health, widowhood and sexuality; and
8. respect and ageing.

Two hundred women were interviewed for the survey. For both communities interviews were done, in most instances, in the respondent's home without the presence of others. This was not always easy, especially in the homes of the August Town women, where quite often there were a number of curious relatives. However, their curiosity was circumvented by moving the interview to the verandah of their house, if it had one, or by sitting outside the house.

Case Studies

Twenty-five of the women who participated in the survey were visited four to five times over the course of the fieldwork, and the information obtained from them in addition to the material from the structured interviews form the substance for the case studies,[16] some of which are to be found dispersed throughout the book as complete case studies; in other places extracts are used as quotations. The case studies were used to explore, *inter alia*, issues of work and family and the power relationships in the lives of women from midlife on as they lived out their lives in Jamaican society. The names used in the case studies and elsewhere in the text are all fictitious.

The women of the case studies were chosen primarily because they were willing to allow themselves to be revisited and to have more detailed discussions about their lives. The case studies proved to be an invaluable part of the research methodology in that the women were prepared not only to answer questions about sensitive and less sensitive issues, but also to elaborate in such ways as to enable me to better understand their situations. The case studies allowed me to build rapport and to gain the confidence of the women even more than during the initial interviews, allowing me to get closer to the realities of their lives: the frustrations, the struggles and the triumphs. In essence, the repeat visits required for the case studies allowed me to capture something of the complexities of the lives of the respondents, the framework of power relationships, the ambivalence in the discourse surrounding women's lives and the subtleties and contradictions that were very much a part of these women's everyday reality. The vacillations of the woman who allowed her two adult, professional daughters to continue to live at home and largely ignore much of the economic responsibilities entailed in running a home, while she hoped daily that they would move on to their own independent existence, was one good example of this contradiction (see chapter 3). The case studies were especially valuable with regard to analysis of the parent–offspring relations, giving it greater depth and meaning. And although the findings did not contradict the nature of the relationships disclosed during the interviews, they suggested that they were not nearly as harmonious as the interviews alone would lead us to conclude.

The Perception Questionnaire

Implicit in this research study was the issue of how women in midlife and older are perceived by the broader society. The problem that faced me methodologically was how to unearth this perception. A number of different possibilities as to how I could do this were suggested by my review of past experience, such as a survey of the folklore, popular literature and newspapers to see how women of this age group are portrayed. I decided, however, that the best way I could establish these perceptions would be to have conversations about such women with the following persons:

1. some of their relatives of varying ages;
2. some younger persons (non-relatives);
3. civil servants who deal with women from midlife, such as post office workers;
4. pension officers;
5. male and female health workers of all age groups; and
6. trade unionists.

Fifty such interviews were done, which addressed issues directly relating to how older women were perceived by family and society. The perception questionnaire embodied eight questions and took approximately five to ten minutes to complete. The questions asked are summarized here. The additional questions to policymakers in labour, social security and the trade unions sought to determine these person's perceptions about the role of older women in the labour force; whether they were perceived as a threat to younger workers; whether or not they experienced age-related discrimination and if there were any specific policies that influenced or dictated the treatment of older women in the workforce. The main research questions asked specifically of health personnel and policymakers addressed the question of whether or not middle-aged and older women were seen as a special group requiring health care.

The trade unionists spoke of women of this age group as hard-working and dependable. They did not perceive them to be a threat to younger workers, and stated that there were no specific policies to guide the treatment of older women in the workplace. The responses in relation to health (see also chapter 5) were that women of this age group were not seen as a special group in need of health care.

The leads that I found in relation to the perceptions encouraged me to find and explore the discourses of older women, from which the perceptions had arisen. Some of the discourses were identified and form an integral part of this book, enabling a better understanding of the lives of older women.

In summary, the research revealed that there was not only one discourse on specific issues relating to women's lives, but that there was first of all the dominant discourse and then other discourses. For example, in the situation of family life, the data showed that there were many contradictions in the discourses. It is believed, for example, that women are taken care of by their children when they grow older. This was not always the case. The discourse to which women subscribed was that they would continue to "do" for their children and other relatives, even as older women. There were many discourses, and in some cases women acted in accord with the discourses, while in other instances they demonstrated ambivalence and resistance to them. Another important point about the various discourses on women's lives was that in some instances the dominant discourses were close to those the literature presents about the lives of First World women of this age group, and were not the lived experiences of Jamaican women, especially working-class women.

CONCLUSION

This book seeks to provide information on this important but relatively unresearched topic in the Caribbean. The new knowledge highlights intellectual and theoretical issues not previously raised and so should contribute to the literature on women. In particular it demonstrates the inadequacy of existing conceptions of "power" in explaining the situation of this group of older women. Discursive powers are seen to be at play in relation to Jamaican midlife and older women. Cheerful as well as reluctant conformity is evidenced by the women themselves, sometimes as a rather puzzled resistance, in that they are resisting but ambivalent about their resistance.

These women were, in the end, a source of great encouragement to this researcher. They stated that they thought that this type of research was long overdue, especially in light of the enormous economic difficulties and dislocations, which they argued were being caused by structural adjustment programmes, deregulation and devaluation. They stated that they feared that the changes in the economic management of the country were affecting their role in cushioning the effects of these policies on their family. They were pleased that someone was concerned about their lives, their welfare, their problems, their work, how they were viewed in the society, their power or powerlessness, both at the micro and the macro levels, and, most of all, how they were coping in a changing society. It is hoped that this research will draw attention to this group, "midlife and older women", and that the society will become more responsive in terms of its obligations to them as a group.

Chapter 1 describes the social and economic environment during the period under review. Chapter 2 looks at family life, exploring the relationships in which middle-aged and older women are involved. Many important issues are raised, which include familial interdependence and sexuality. In chapter 3, the issue of paid and unpaid work in the life of middle-aged and older women within the formal and informal sectors is explored and the societal expectations about work for women of this age group are analysed. The health of women of the age group under discussion is the focus of chapter 4, and the issue of the response of the health-care system to the needs of older women is explored. Chapter 5 discusses the incidence of widowhood in Jamaican society, the problems women encounter when their husbands or partners die and the mechanisms they adopt for coping with these problems. The ambivalence that exists in the discourse surrounding widowhood is also discussed. In the conclusion, the most crucial results of the research are highlighted, especially in relation to the unrecognized contribution of women beyond midlife. It is here that conclusions are drawn and suggestions for possible action for the future are made.

CHAPTER 1
THE SOCIAL AND
ECONOMIC ENVIRONMENT OF THE STUDY

INTRODUCTION

This chapter presents a picture of the social and economic environment in Jamaica in 1990–91 when the research for this book was done. Although this book is primarily about the life and work of women aged fifty to seventy-four years and the framework of power in which they operated in Jamaica, it would hardly be possible to appreciate their true situation without an overview of the "real" social and economic existence of women and men in the larger society. Therefore, reference is now made to issues that were affecting the broader society at the time. We recognize that although these women lived within a framework of power in which they responded to the societal expectations of them, they were also influenced by the realities of their relationships with their families, communities and the state which impacted upon their lives.

Jamaica is the largest English-speaking island and the third largest country in the Caribbean. It has a total land area of 4,411 square miles (11,424 square kilometres). The island is situated to the southwest of Miami, Florida, in the United States, and can be reached in an hour and a half by air. The island is divided into three counties and fourteen parishes. Two of the parishes, Kingston, the capital, and St Andrew, are adjacent and are administered economically as one. The population of Kingston and St Andrew was estimated to be 600,000 in 1990.[1]

Two years prior to its independence from Britain in 1962, Jamaica had a population of 1.6 million, according to the 1960 census. Since that time it has seen significant population growth, and had a population of 2.4 million at the end of 1990 and 2.62 million at the end of 2002. However, since independence, efforts have been made to contain population growth through the work of the National Family Planning Board and the Family Planning Association of Jamaica. Additionally, as Jamaican women have become more educated they have seen for themselves the benefits of smaller families; consequently, the fertility rate for Jamaica has fallen from 5.54 in 1970 to 2.90 in 1989 and to 2.4 in 2001 (PAHO 2001).

Jamaica has a youthful population, with almost half of the population (44.7 per cent) being less than twenty years old in 1990.[2] Since the 1970s the declining fertility rates have begun to make an important difference in age structure (UNICEF/Planning Institute of Jamaica 1991, 3). The population pyramid now exhibits a narrowing base, which is indicative of a maturing population. On the other hand, mortality rates have declined steadily since the 1920s, with the crude death rate being 6 per cent in 1989 and the life expectancy being seventy years for men and seventy-two years for women (UNICEF/Planning Institute of Jamaica 1991, 6).[3] The importance of this decline in mortality rate is that the population is ageing, which means that provision will have to be made by family and the state for the employment and later the care of a larger group of older people than was formerly the case.

The age structure of the population as it was during the period under consideration may be summarized as follows. In 1990, the population under fourteen years comprised 33.3 per cent, the working age population (fifteen to sixty-four years) represented 59.1 per cent, and the elderly, sixty-five years and over, constituted 7.6 per cent. Women fifty to seventy-four years old were approximately 12 per cent (142,940) of the total female population in 1990.

THE ECONOMY

Jamaica, like the other anglophone countries of the Caribbean, was colonized by Britain. This experience was one in which Jamaica supplied the "mother country"[4] with products such as sugar, bananas, bauxite, coffee, cocoa, cotton, logwood and pimento, among other items of raw material. The economy of Jamaica up to the early 1990s was still structured around the production of primary goods for export. The continuation of this pattern in the 1990s ensured that Jamaica remained unable to achieve economic stability, growth and wealth.

The late 1960s and 1970s was a period of relative prosperity for Jamaica, primarily because of the high price of bauxite on the world market. Higher sugar prices, which rose briefly, to Jamaica's advantage, following the US embargo of Cuba after the Cuban revolution, and migration to the United Kingdom and United States, which led to increased remittances to local people from relatives abroad, were advantageous factors for the economy during this period. Remittances continued to be important to the Jamaican economy into the 1990s. In an article in the *Sunday Gleaner* on 4 August 1991, Professor Bernard Headley, a respected US-based Jamaican political scientist, stated that "steady remittances from us [US-based Jamaicans] into their new tax-free A and B accounts have moved the two savings programmes ahead of the country's sugar and banana industries in foreign exchange earnings after less than a year of operation".[5] His article was pointing to the importance of these remittances not only to individual family members but to the economy as a whole. The importance of remittances from relatives continues to be important to the Jamaican economy.

By the early 1970s, Jamaica's economy was under stress mainly because of the increased price of oil on the world market, which elevated prices for almost all imported goods locally. Jamaica depends heavily on imported items not only for food consumption but also for the operation of factories and other businesses. By 1973, due to international developments in the alumina industry[6] and the rise in the cost of energy after 1973, Jamaican bauxite became less competitive on the world market and those seeking to buy turned to cheaper sources, such as Australia, Brazil and West Africa. Thereafter, the Jamaican economy declined almost continuously until the end of 1980 (Levitt 1991, 11).

In an effort to seek assistance for its financial difficulties the government entered into an agreement with the International Monetary Fund (IMF). The country's economic problems did not disappear, but appeared to have worsened, as is described by Girvan, Bernal and Hughes (1980, 2) in the following comment:

> IMF stabilization policies in the Caribbean in the 1980s have generally compounded the economic crisis, a conclusion that is particularly well illustrated in the case of Jamaica. The Manley government signed an IMF agreement in April 1977, after the international banks responding to US pressures stopped granting credit to Jamaica. The conditions for this two-year IMF agreement required Jamaica to devalue its currency, impose higher taxes, and reduce public expenditure. The IMF cancelled the agreement in December of that year, accusing the Manley government of non compliance. It then required even more drastic conditions in subsequent negotiations, terms which Jamaica was forced to accept in 1978, and when implemented, contributed to the fall of the Manley government.

The IMF stabilization policies in Jamaica, instead of bringing stability, which the people desperately needed, led to devaluation of the dollar, and the resulting higher prices wreaked havoc on the lives of the people, especially the poor who are the majority, and contributed to rising unemployment. Unemployment increased from 21 per cent in 1975 to 27 per cent in 1980 (ECLAC 1984, 251).

WOMEN AND STRUCTURAL ADJUSTMENT

During the period under discussion, the words "structural adjustment" became a part of the everyday language of the Jamaican population. Structural adjustment refers to a particular set of changes countries requiring loans from international lending agencies have to make in their economies. These changes are aimed at restoring financial stability, balance of payments equilibrium and economic growth to economically troubled countries, and are linked to specific conditions and requirements that are dictated to the governments by the IMF and other international financial institutions. These conditions are invariably regarded as austere by governments and the people.

It has been argued that women who are heads of household are particularly affected negatively by the effects of structural adjustment. Antrobus (1987) for example, argued that some of the policies have been so damaging to low-income households that it is clear that they have failed to take women into consideration. In Jamaica, structural adjustment removed a number of benefits previously provided by the state. By shifting more responsibility for survival from the state to the household, structural adjustment policies increased the burden on the poor, especially women.

Many of the damaging changes occasioned by structural adjustment took place in relation to the provision of health, education and social services, and where these fell short, it was left to women to try to ensure that their families received services, which at times was impossible because they were unable to meet the cost of these services. Davies and Anderson (1987, 1) argue that "the economic crisis has made it extremely difficult for families to survive on a single wage, forcing additional women into the labour force to meet the rising cost of living and the decreased wage earning capacity of men due to unemployment or wage cuts, or due to their absence as a result of migration".

The burden of the increases in the cost of health, education and social services was not the only problem with which women had to contend. The amount of money that the government was prepared to spend on housing, water and electricity fell dramatically in real terms and, in some instances, reduced government expenditure was also accompanied by increased prices. Government water rates increased by 55 per cent in 1984, and pressure in the housing market caused significant increases in the price of housing. House prices in the rural area, over the period January 1981 to June 1985, increased by 115 per cent, while increases in the cost of housing in the Kingston and St Andrew areas was 95 per cent (Antrobus 1989, 6).

This research shows older women were severely disadvantaged by the policies of structural adjustment, as they tended to struggle not only for their own economic survival but also for that of their adult offspring twenty-five to forty years old and more, and were busy securing and allocating whatever resources, financial or otherwise, that were necessary to make ends meet for their immediate family as well as for extended family, as we see in chapter 2.

The Jamaican economy changed dramatically during the lifetime of these women who are the focus of this research. According to Davies and Anderson (1987) in urban areas, poor women felt the effects of various adjustment policies to a greater extent than most other groups. The adjustment policies, in particular devaluation, resulted in high levels of inflation, affecting especially the price of food. The cost of living increases had come about mainly as a result of the devaluation of the Jamaican dollar, which had been J$1.78 to US$1.00 in November 1983 and had devalued to J$6.40 to US$1.00 in October 1985, J$10.00 to

US$1.00 in May 1991 and J$22.00 to US$1.00 by the end of 1991, and all this in a situation where wages had not changed for the majority in the society.

The inflation rate continued to rise and was 80.2 per cent towards the end of 1991.[7] Life became much more difficult not only for working-class women, but for the majority of women and especially for older women who were on pensions or fixed incomes. The increasing cost of living along with the high level of unemployment, it is argued, had the effect of worsening the crime situation in Kingston. Older women, who are more vulnerable to numerous pressures in the society because of their age, were further oppressed by having to guard themselves against thieves entering their yards and homes and doing damage not only to property in an effort to enter the house, but also, in their efforts to steal, committing violent acts against the women. The case studies make special reference to comments women made about their fears of being robbed and of having to lose sleep by being vigilant at night instead of sleeping soundly.

However, these women, like so many other women in the society in 1990–91 had found ways of surviving what clearly was a social and economic crisis in Jamaica at the time. It appears that they drew closer to their family and their community in recognition that scarce resources serve best when they are pooled. Perhaps the best example of pooled resources is seen in working-class as well as in middle-class communities, where household sizes were reported to be growing and very few older women were living alone (Statistical Institute of Jamaica 1989).

THE HEALTH SECTOR

"Among countries of comparable income, Jamaica has long enjoyed an enviable record in the provision of health and educational services" (Levitt 1991, 49). There were, however, significant changes that set the country back for perhaps decades as a result of the economic adjustments in the 1980s.[8] We are told that "real per capita outlays on health declined from US$44 per capita in 1982/83 to US$25.6 by 1986/87 – a reduction of 42 percent" (Levitt 1991, 50).

Capital expenditure for health declined dramatically all through the 1980s, resulting in a situation in which hospitals could not be maintained and rehabilitated as in the past. The high cost of imported drugs and the removal of some subsidies led to shortages of drugs and medical supplies in the public health service. Prior to this, there were very few costs that had to be paid by those receiving care in the health sector financed by the state. But with structural adjustment, the government introduced "a wide-based system of charges for services offered at the public hospitals and health centres, which had previously been free" (Cornia, Jolly and Stewart 1987).

Workers in the health service became demoralized as a result of their poor wages and working conditions. There was a mass exodus at all levels of health personnel during the 1980s, including large numbers of doctors and nurses. Apart from those who chose to leave for better opportunities, under structural adjustment there was also a large-scale retrenchment of health workers and the abolition of several posts in 1985. All of these factors led to a significant deterioration of the public health service, leaving it unable to adequately provide health care for the population.

The shortage of labour in the health service continued into the 1990s, but in an effort to stem the outward flow of nurses, the government doubled salaries from J$18,751 to J$30,753, plus allowances (Levitt 1991). Despite this initiative on the part of the government, the shortage remained a reality and patients, even women in labour, were often left unattended (Sargent and Rawlins 1991).

One important and damaging aspect of the deterioration of services in the public health sector was that more people sought care within the private health sector, although the costs were prohibitive for those on low incomes. The *Survey of Living Conditions* (Statistical Institute of Jamaica 1989) showed 55 per cent of the population attending private doctors for health care, although the cost was in excess of J$50 per visit.[9] That would have been more than the poor could really afford to pay, and must have left many unable to provide food and other necessities because of what had to be spent on health care.

NATIONAL INSURANCE

In addition to health and educational services, in 1990–91 there were other state provisions available to the Jamaican population, some of which bear special relevance to the situation of midlife and older women. State provisions were available through the National Insurance Scheme (NIS), which is a contributory system of social security that offers some financial protection to workers and their families against loss of income arising from injury on the job, sickness, old age and death of the bread winner. The benefits provided under the NIS in 1990–91 were old age, invalidity, widows, widowers, orphans and special children, employment injury, maternity allowance and funeral grants.[10] The rules for qualifying for these benefits were quite complex (Jamaica Information Service 1990).

The old-age benefits were available as a pension, allowance[11] or grant.[12] Those eligible for the old-age pension were men sixty-five years and over and women sixty years and over who had made the required NIS contributions and had retired. If the person eligible for the benefit remained in full-time employment then the benefit would not be paid. However, on reaching the age of seventy for men and sixty-five for women, even if he or she remained in full-time employment the contributor was deemed to be retired and the benefit would be paid.[13]

Prior to October 1991, women were eligible to receive only one of the two main benefits, but after that time women became eligible to receive the two benefits, that is, the one for herself, widow's pension, as well as her husband's pension from her husband's contribution. Prior to this, the issue had been a vexed one, as a woman so eligible would only have received one pension: the larger of the two benefits for which she had qualified. Most often the two would be very similar, and the woman would be no better off. She might, therefore, receive her own pension, but no widow's pension.

The economy continued in 1991 to experience serious social and economic difficulties, and members of the population, including some midlife and older women, continued to manage despite grave odds. Older women were able to cope by continuing to work even up to the age of seventy years in the formal as well as the informal sector, by pooling their resources and by rendering assistance to their relatives and members of their community. This pooling of resources no doubt was done in the hope that there would be reciprocal benefits.

It would seem, though, that the more strategies the women devised for surviving, the greater were the pressures and the burdens that were placed on them by the society. The picture presented was one in which it appeared that the government recognized that it did not need to help those women, as they continued to be able to find means of helping themselves, no matter how desperate the situation. It is perhaps with this type of situation in mind that Deere (1990, 71) states that by providing a retreat from an exploitative system, Caribbean forms of the family and community also facilitate the continuation of exploitation and the inequitable distribution of resources. It appears that governments have in fact taken advantage of women's ability to draw on traditional networks of support to introduce policies which have been particularly devastating to women and those for whose care they have been traditionally responsible: children and the elderly.

CONCLUSION

Midlife and older women in the study undoubtedly showed the importance of the role of older women in the society, by being able to cope when their menfolk and children were unemployed, and when the government appeared to be less than sensitive to their needs and unable to provide much help. These Jamaican women were not finding Jamaica an easy place to live in 1990–91. The picture that was presented was one in which the economic changes that had taken place since the early 1960s were having the most devastating effects on their lives. These women, especially those of the working class and lower middle class, were trying to cope but were having grave economic difficulties and feared that, as they grew older, their economic situation would be more seriously threatened as they were not now in a position to save for the future.

CHAPTER 2
FAMILY AND POWER

I have three children alive, two live abroad and the third lives here with me. Her marriage is in difficulty at present, so that is why she has returned home. I have never married and never planned to have any of these children but now more than thirty years later I'm glad that I had the three of them because I worked hard with them and they have made me very proud.
— *Interview with Respondent no. 2*

My mother was diabetic and lost her sight. She lived with me and my family for ten years until she died a year ago. I was glad that my children [two daughters] were able to grow up in a home which had a senior member, as it is important in a family for children to learn from experience about the care of older people.
— *Interview with Respondent no. 139*

INTRODUCTION

This chapter analyses family life and the power relations that midlife and older women experienced daily as both subjects and objects of power. This analysis is done in relation to the assumption that such women live out their lives in a framework of power where family and community do not fully recognize their efforts nor provide them with the necessary support to effect the various tasks that they carry out for family and community. In order to understand these power relations a number of issues around which there are cultural expectations for the family will be explored. First, the perception of women of this age group by family and community will be analysed. The interdependence that operated between those women and their relatives and how this affected their economic situation will be explored. Special attention will be paid to the issue of remittances from relatives abroad, and the connection between this and issues of migration in the lives of those older women. The phenomenon of migration affects the obligations of such women and the support given to them. The relationships those women experienced with their various family members will also be explored, noting the differences and similarities by class.

The argument pursued in this chapter is that despite all that those women did for family within the home and outside the home as income earners, they were not perceived as economically important, but as caregivers by their families and by the community. I will also argue that women were pivotal to the family, and that family depended on them even as they grew older, and that whereas cultural expectations were important in the ways in which women lived their lives, other factors such as the increasing cost of living, high rental, unemployment and migration among their relatives, generally influenced their daily experiences.

The chapter is organized in a number of sections. The first provides an overview of some of the discussions that have surrounded the family and household in general, and the Caribbean family and household specifically, over the past four decades. Other sections, drawing on the data from the survey and case studies, look at midlife and older women and their relationship with their families, noting the differences and similarities by class. The final section draws some conclusions about power relations and family life for midlife and older women.

FAMILY AND HOUSEHOLD: AN OVERVIEW

The family and the household are two of the main institutions in which women midlife and older interact. It is within families that major areas of socialization take place, and it is here that individuals first begin to internalize the culture. Here daughters and sons learn what society expects of them in relation to their parents and what they will be expected to do as young adults. Here they observe the relationships between their parents and grandparents and learn what ageing parents might expect of them and also what they can expect of those parents.

As a concept, the family is one that has been much abused, misunderstood, and about which there has been much vagueness. Barrett (1980, 199) argues that the family does not exist other than as an ideological construct, since the structure of the household, definition and meaning of kinship and the ideology of the "family" itself have all varied enormously in different types of society. I would agree with Barrett that family varies a great deal in all societies, not least of all in Jamaican society, in which household members who are not consanguineous or consensually related may even be more closely related emotionally and socially than members of the so-called nuclear family. The family and the household are distinct and separate entities, the household being a co-residential unit. Both terms have their uses in describing social reality. However, at times it is difficult to differentiate one from the other, and not all Caribbean sociologists and anthropologists do.

The Jamaican family is so diverse that conventional definitions do not meet my understanding of it. The family in Jamaica is not simply the nuclear family but includes at times such members as might be found in a nuclear family or have some such members absent and include other members as might be found in an extended family. Clarke (1957), for example, identified twelve different family types. The diversity found in the Jamaican family arises as a result of the history of the region in which female-headed households were the norm during slavery and in the immediate post-emancipation period. In more recent times, the economic condition of the society that has led to large bouts of out-migration has also contributed to the variety in family forms that are seen in Jamaica. For me, the family is a group of persons who consider themselves related by blood or marriage (legal or common-law), who may or may not live together and will include some who live not only outside the family residence but outside the community and indeed outside of the island. My definition reflects the realities of family life as it is seen not only in Jamaica but also in the wider Caribbean. Deere (1990, 70) refers to this diversity also: "For the majority of the black, working-class population of the Caribbean, the concept of family often extends beyond the household unit of nuclear family, beyond the neighbourhood or village and even beyond the country, to encompass a network of mutually supporting members."

The Caribbean family has been the focus of many theorists since the 1940s. Not too much time will be devoted here to the conceptualizations of the Caribbean family over these several decades, as these have been well documented.[1] Three main approaches have been used in the literature to explain the structure, composition and function of the Caribbean family. These approaches are now dated but are mentioned because of their historical importance in the study of Caribbean families: the cultural diffusion approach, the social pathology approach and the structural functional approach.[2] These various approaches have had their supporters, converts and critics over time. They have at least one thing in common, and that is that they all take "Anglo-American" family norms to be a standard against which other people's differences are measured. Thus, they are all ethnocentric.

From the various theoretical approaches to the Caribbean family we have come to associate Caribbean women with concepts such as matrifocal or "mother centred", whereas the term "marginal" has been used for decades to describe the Caribbean male. In more recent years, the term "female-headed" has been used increasingly in the description of some Caribbean families. See for example, Massiah (1983) and Louet, Grosh and Van der Gaag (1993), who highlight the situation of female-headed households and families in the Caribbean, estimate the frequency of the phenomenon and focus on some of the problems encountered by these women and their children daily.

The term "matrifocal", as it has been used for the Caribbean family, means that the activities of the family centre around the mother. It does not only mean female-headed, single parent in the Caribbean, but has a different usage from that which is commonly found in the social science literature.[3] The mother is very important to the family. She makes important social, political and economic decisions concerning the family; she is quite often in a favourable relationship with her children, compared to the relationships that they have with other family members, and they look to her as a source of stability and control.

Women are able to exercise power through a vast range of societal situations. For example, as mothers, women are able to exercise power over their children, to determine some aspects of their children's destiny, for example, which schools they will attend, if they will attend school at all, and whether or not the children will be allowed to maintain contact with their fathers and the father's family if the father is not co-resident. In Jamaica, the status of motherhood, as a result of the discourse on motherhood, is normally highly respected and is certainly sought after among women (Roberts and Sinclair 1978; Mohammed and Perkins 1999). As this chapter shows, motherhood also confers some elements of power in that while it is not always insurance for old age, in many instances, it will be advantageous to the future. So women have power in their being mothers, as well as in their capability of being mothers.

THE PERCEPTION OF OLDER WOMEN BY FAMILY AND COMMUNITY

In the annual Jamaican theatrical production, the pantomime, the older woman is typically presented as someone who is left behind to take care of children whose relatives are abroad or living in the "city". Like all good pantomimes, the Jamaican production reflects popular culture. Media presentations and everyday societal discussions also portray older women in this role. The perception questionnaire referred to in the introduction was used to see if family members of the women in the sample and members of their community shared this view.

Although more than half of the women in each of the communities worked for an income, they were not perceived as workers by their family and community. They were seen primarily as mothers, grandmothers and, less frequently, as advisers.[4] When asked about the main roles that they thought women from midlife played in the society, no one saw them as "workers" primarily. They were seen mainly as mothers, grandmothers and caregivers,[5] and although these designations were associated with various tasks, these tasks were not seen as work by the relatives and other respondents to the perception questionnaire. Fifty-seven per cent saw mothering as the main role, while 22 per cent saw grandmothering as the main role. Absolutely no one saw the main role for midlife and older women as "worker", that is paid worker, but 16 per cent saw paid employment as the third most important role of women in this age group. Although an average of 64 per cent of these women worked for an income,[6] to their relatives and immediate community, their mothering and grandmothering roles, that is to say their work within the home, were seen as more important. In these roles they impacted more directly and importantly on the lives of the people immediately around them. The fact that they were able to do this more advantageously because they worked outside of the home, and had incomes, was not taken into account. Older women in this discourse were constituted primarily as caregivers. The respondents also saw these women as caregivers and teachers and upholders of moral standards and values in the society. Nonetheless, in whatever role they saw these women, most declared that these roles were very important to the society.

EXPLORING FAMILY RELATIONSHIPS: ASPECTS OF ECONOMIC AND SOCIAL INTERDEPENDENCE

In order to better understand the relationship that the women of this study had with their various family members, we need to discuss the issue of "current union status". In Jamaica, middle-class women are more likely to be married than are working-class women at every point of the life cycle.[7] Some working-class women who have not married by middle age tend to terminate their common-law relationships. Married women of this older age group usually stay married; divorces are rare in this group and if there is a separation, it is usually informal. Analysis of the union status of the women in the survey reveals the same pattern, which is class related but not class discrete.[8]

Almost all of the women in the middle-class community (Hope Pastures), that is 90 per cent, had been married at one time or another, compared with 48 per cent of the women in the working-class community (August Town). The data indicate that 41 per cent of the August Town sample and 61 per cent of the Hope Pastures sample were married or in a common-law relationship at the time of the survey.

What women do for their families will be influenced by whether or not they are the heads of their families. From the data available, we note that in both communities, women represented just less than a half of heads of households.[9] Readers should be reminded though, that a female head of household in the Jamaican context does not necessarily mean a single woman. This was confirmed by Louet, Grosh and Van der Gagg (1993), who provide evidence of male partners living in the homes of women who saw themselves as heads of household. In this study, 43 per cent of the August Town women and 45 per cent of the Hope Pastures women were heads of household, and 33 per cent and 49 per cent for August Town and Hope Pastures, respectively, reported themselves as spouse or partner of the head of household.

The Caribbean region has a relatively high percentage of women as heads of households and Jamaica ranks among the highest. The 1982 Census (Statistical

Institute of Jamaica 1982) showed female heads of households in the labour force as 47.5 per cent for Jamaica; 33.1 per cent for Trinidad and Tobago, and 46.8 per cent for Barbados. Massiah (1983, 56) notes that "one of the groups most readily identifiable and most vulnerable to poverty is that group of women who head households". Data for Jamaica on women as heads of household (Planning Institute of Jamaica 1985) showed 35 per cent of all Jamaican households having women as heads, and this percentage was even higher (45 per cent) for the Kingston Metropolitan Area. In the two communities studied here, the percentage of women as heads of household was very similar. Not much has changed since 1985 and women remain of great consequence in terms of household headship.

RELATIONSHIP WITH SPOUSE OR PARTNER

The case study data and the survey were revealing about the relationship that women had with their spouses and partners and, in particular, threw light on the tension between their acknowledged work of caregiving and their unacknowledged work as provider. The in-depth interviews provided by the case studies additionally showed a situation in which those working-class women who lived with partners did not expect the spouse to do very many things around the house, or outside the house for that matter. They showed themselves to be very resourceful. They did not expect their menfolk to do anything for them that they could do for themselves. Some of this was borne out by the survey, which examined the day-to-day relationship that women had experienced with their spouse or partner. The double-edged nature of this type of relationship needs to be acknowledged, as these women's resourcefulness gave them skills and knowledge of their autonomy, but also left men in a privileged position of being "looked after".

The research sought to explore the practical and day-to-day relationship experienced by midlife and older women with their spouse or partner; relationships that addressed the issue of power, how it was used, and how it manifested itself in daily activities within these women's households. Because I was aware that there would be fewer husbands or partners than there were women in the sample, I sought information not only about their current relationship but also the relationship the women had experienced with their partners up to the point of separation, for those who were no longer in a relationship. It was my hope that the responses about the sorts of familial activities, the division of labour in the home and social activities in which these women and their partners participated would lead to an understanding of their relationships and the part reciprocal power played in these relationships.

Women, from both community samples, who were in good health and available to do the shopping were expected by their spouses and other family members to do it.[10] They were expected to do all or most of the cooking and most of the jobs around the house. In fact, it was probably the women who themselves decided to do the shopping, because this would mean that they had some amount of control over the funds used to finance the shopping venture. They could then decide how much to spend, how much to hold back for special projects and how much to put aside or use for their "partner".[11] Further light on this aspect of financial control is shed by examining who paid the bills, who did banking transactions and who was responsible, for instance, if there was need for house maintenance and repair.

The data reveal that, whereas in both groups more than three quarters of the women were expected to do the shopping, less than half in each group was expected to take responsibility for the banking transactions. This was probably influenced by who was "bringing in the money". It would seem that men often organized their familial responsibilities in such a way that major financial transactions remained in their domain. This was not because older women were incapable of dealing with major financial institutions, because that was certainly not the case in Jamaica in 1990–91, but because women of this age group had come from that generation in which the societal expectation was that women should defer to men and allow men to appear to be the ones in charge, at least in public. Other data available in the study showed that half of the working-class women and one third of the middle-class women had responsibility for banking transactions.

It is important to understand not only the nature of the power relations as they were manifested in the division of labour between these women and their spouses, but also to know how women felt about these divisions. Were they content to have the tasks apportioned as they were or would they have preferred another ordering of things? It appeared that these women took for granted a division of labour that might have appeared to work to their disadvantage. The respondents gave the impression that they did what they did, because, to quote them, "Others will not do." It appeared that they were often unable to convince spouses to do some tasks and so went ahead and did what was necessary.

This suggests they might have preferred something else. Perhaps they so much took for granted the existing state of affairs that they had not given any serious thought to an alternative. The spouses here demonstrated their power by not making themselves available to do too many tasks.

The case study that follows was not unique and shows a woman who had internalized the societal belief that Jamaican women cannot manage their lives if they are not in a close relationship with a man. Although, as we will see later, there was resistance among some widows to this constitution of them, there is an extremely common saying and belief in Jamaica: "Every woman needs a fadah."[12] This does not mean that women need a biological father constantly around them, but that women need to have men to "look out for them", to avoid being taken advantage of. So, although there were several aspects of her relationship with her husband that might seem unsatisfactory, this woman disregarded them and was very effective in organizing the economic and other aspects of her family life.

Case No. 1

Mrs Ulett, one of the working-class respondents from August Town, was fifty years old and married. She had married at the age of nineteen, and stated that given another chance she would not marry young. Unlike most of the women in the lower socio-economic group, Mrs Ulett had the benefit of secondary education. She had attended one of the better girls' schools in Kingston, but left without obtaining any educational certificates. Her husband worked as a driver for a furniture company but did not possess a motor vehicle of his own.

The couple had no children of their own, as the child she had died at birth and serious gynaecological problems had left her unable to have children. She had, however, been totally responsible for the care of her niece who, at the time of the interviews, was ten years old. The child was her brother's daughter. He had died in a car accident when the child was a year old. The natural mother had abandoned the child upon the father's death.

Mrs Ulett, unlike many other women, decided that she would never do domestic work. She had been self-employed in the "selling trade" all of her working life.

She lived in a one-room apartment with her husband and her niece, whom she described as her "daughter". The room was in a large house, which had been subdivided and tenanted out as a number of self-contained rooms. Her room was crowded, but tidy. The bed was the major item, while there was also a huge refrigerator (fifteen cubic feet), a dining table and a gas cooker in one corner. Her husband, she said, had been a difficult person ever since they married, but she coped with her family by minding her daughter, spending a significant portion of her entire earnings on the child's education, and by ignoring her husband's consistent infidelity. "He brings his money home though, and pays the bills and the rent. We don't want for anything around here, so I don't bother to say anything to him these days," she said.

In relation to family, she spoke very kindly of her mother: "One in a million. She has been very good; a positive influence on me." Her mother, then seventy years old, lived nearby and Mrs Ulett had some responsibilities for her care.

Mrs Ulett attributed her success at managing her life to her good health, the support of her church, and the fact that she was able to relate to her husband despite the "problems" as she referred to them. In terms of her family life, she said she coped because she did not allow what her husband did to bother her.

"Life is hard, but I will not complain," she said. She hoped to keep ahead economically through her "selling". She sold ice, "suck-suck", [13] soft drinks, other ice products and beer. She said, "Business is not always steady; some days, some weeks I make some money and at other times I don't make any money." On average she made about J$800 per month.

Her niece helped her with the selling when she was not in school. The child appeared lively and bright and Mrs Ulett said that the child's ambition was to become a doctor. She was very proud of the child, who had recently taken the Common Entrance Examination.[14]

Mrs Ulett complained about the high cost of living, noting that school books for her daughter had been J$1,000 for that year. She also complained that the cost of a small cylinder of cooking gas had risen from J$2.50, ten years previously, to J$70 in January 1991. Even extra classes for the Common Entrance Examination had increased to J$20, for Saturday classes only.

During the time I visited Mrs Ulett over the fieldwork period, her landlord gave her family notice to leave the house. Her rent at the time was J$50 per month. After several months of house hunting, she was unsuccessful in finding accommodation similar in price to her accustomed rent and eventually settled for two rooms, in a house without electricity, for J$200 per month. She was sorry to have to move house as she had lived at that particular location for twenty years and knew many people. She stated that she "did not mix much", but that she was respected by the people of the community.

Mrs Ulett spent a great deal of her spare time caring for an elderly woman in the community but complained about the stinginess of the family members of the old woman, who were reluctant to reimburse her the money she spent on bus fares to visit the elderly lady when she was hospitalized.

Her relationship with her mother, her niece and her elderly neighbour for whom she provided care attested to her acceptance of the caregiving role that is accorded to women of this age group. She had respect from the community because of her caring relationship with her niece, because of her relationship with the church, and her helpfulness to an elderly woman in the community. This respect was very important to her.

The data provided information about the social activities in which women and their menfolk participated together. The main social activities in which women of this age group became involved were attending church, visiting relatives, visiting friends and attending community and other social functions. The data indicate that there was a good deal of participation in various activities between the women and their spouses, especially among the middle-class women of the sample. This might suggest that these women felt more comfortable with their spouses outside their homes than did the women of the working-class community. Conversely, it could be that, whereas middle-class women and men have more social activities in common and are concerned for those around them to know that they have interests in such activities, working-class men have fewer social interests in common with women of their own class and so spend their spare time in different activities. It is well documented that working-class men in Jamaica like to spend their time visiting their friends and also pass the time chatting outside shops and bars. These men exercise their power by staying out of their homes as much as they choose. Women of the age group that is the focus of this study would not have been outside shops "chatting". Naturally there would have been some working-class men who preferred not to be outside of their yards, and who would spend their spare time at home with their family. These, quite often, would be the religious ones, whose pattern of family relationship might be different from those who did not have church activities in common with other members of their family. The above

Midlife and Older Women

demonstrates something of a paradox, in that middle-class marital relations demonstrate more sharing, but a greater degree of female dependence.

CHILDREN IN THEIR HOMES

Women shared their homes with their daughters and sons and also occasionally lived in the homes of their children. The survey data suggest that these women had very amicable relations with their children. We cannot take it for granted, though, that the women would not have their offspring living with them if the relationship had been otherwise, as the shortage of reasonably priced rental units in Jamaica in 1990–91 rendered a certain amount of house sharing inevitable. The findings here about the reasonably good relations affirmed the findings of an earlier study (Rawlins 1988), which showed that women in two communities similar to the ones reported here were pleased with their relationships with their resident children, with middle-class women expressing slightly more satisfaction with these relationships than working-class women. This additional satisfaction relates to the fact that, although they were resident, the children of the middle-class parents made fewer demands and contributed more financially to the household. However, in this study too, the women of the two communities stated that they were on good terms with their resident children, who were usually helpful around the home. They reported that even their young unemployed sons were helpful and did a range of household chores, including cleaning and cooking. One is not unmindful though that women could speak about relations with their children as being "good", when to the onlooker, it might have appeared as less than good.

Naturally, good relations were not always the case and in some situations what happened in the homes of older women who shared with their offspring could be described as oppressive, as we see in Case no. 9, in chapter 3. That case presents a graphic picture of the type of problem that women could encounter as they shared their household. Although Mrs Gooden (Case no. 9) owned her house and shared it with her daughters, each day was a constant power struggle between her and them. It might be argued that the fact that the daughters were able to continue to live in the home when she would rather they had left, showed them on the plus side of the power equation. One cannot also rule out the possibility that, although this lady declared that she wanted her daughters out of the house, that what she actually "fronted" and declared she wanted, and what she really desired were at variance. It would seem that she allowed them to remain in the home because of her belief that women should always "look out for their children". It could be that she was oppressed by a pervasive discourse that constituted women, not only as caregivers but as people who should give care. Thus, allowing her daughters to stay worked to her advantage, in that she then had the sympathy of the community whose members then "looked out for her" in a number of ways because they felt she was being taken advantage of by her daughters, while she was doing the right thing.

We might ask: what were the reasons, generally speaking, grown offspring needed to live in the parental homes? An important societal reason is that additional housing units are always in very short supply and that rent takes a substantial part of the individual's income, irrespective of the class group to which she or he belongs.

Why Offspring Lived with Respondents

The main reason these offspring still lived in their mother's homes was because the mothers wanted them there for a variety of reasons, and because it was more economical. "More economical" in some instances meant "economically wise", not only for the offspring, but also for the woman herself (54 per cent for August Town and 42 per cent for Hope Pastures), as there were instances in which these midlife and older women lent money to their children – daughters especially – to pay rent. Eventually the mother would decide that she could not afford to pay for the daughter's independence and privacy, and that it would be more feasible economically for the daughter to return to the parental home, although the mother would lose her own independence and privacy. This was an example of the type of sacrifice that mothers were prepared to make for their children. By allowing their grown daughters to return to the parental home, they were effectively relinquishing their own privacy and some of their autonomy.

But what does this type of sacrifice, which women make on behalf of their adult children, indicate about familial relations? The relationships were reciprocal, rather than characterized by dependence in only one direction. The women anticipated they would need their daughters most as they grew older and were no longer able to fend for themselves. Very few expected the state to make provision for them in their old age, as this was not what they had observed as the norm. They recognized that daughters, more than sons, spouses and other relatives, would form an important part of their support group in future years. Thus, we see one source of the power that daughters had. Mothers' sometimes seemingly reverential behaviour towards their daughters was in recognition of their possible need for them in the future. But I would not want to give the impression that older women's assistance to their daughters was a cold-blooded and calculated plan on the mothers' part to attempt to ensure reciprocity from their daughters. That was not how I sensed it. It was much more mothers wanting to do things for daughters who were close to them anyway.

With regard to tasks around the home, it was not that relatives did not help with tasks; it was more that relatives were selective about what they helped such women to do. Of the August Town (working class) and Hope Pastures (middle class) samples, 61 and 70 per cent, respectively, stated that relatives helped with household tasks. Among the August Town sample, the ones most likely to help with tasks were the daughters first, then the husbands, then the sons. The daughters were twice as likely to help as the sons. This is perhaps because these daughters were not in full-time employment and so were more likely to be available to help. Among the Hope Pastures group it was the sons first, followed by the daughters, then the husband who were most likely to help with the household tasks. This might be because the sons who lived at home with their mothers in Hope Pastures were those without children. They did not have to attend to children and so had more time to help with household tasks.

CHILDREN AND OTHER RELATIVES: THE GENERAL SITUATION

One way in which the relationship between these women and their relatives was better understood was through the economic and social interdependence that was their lived reality. Within Jamaican culture it is commonly said that women have children as insurance for the future. It may be argued that some women do agree with this cultural belief and act accordingly. Women do this because they can be assured that there will be someone to help them financially as they grow older, as well as to have someone to take care of them physically. Although this is the belief, there were also contradictions between the discourse and the experienced reality, as we will see later. We should note that few women acknowledged that they had their children as insurance for the future, and that, in reality, women could not rely on their children for financial assistance. Although there were some cases of children giving financial assistance to their mothers, women were of greater financial assistance to their children than was the reverse situation. Some offspring had to return to their mother's home, among both classes, in response to the increasing cost of living in Jamaica in 1990–91. The case below was not an unusual one and makes the point.

Case No. 2

Mrs Young was a youthful looking sixty-two-year-old woman. She had lived in August Town for thirty-three years. She had been living together with her husband for thirty-eight years and they had been married for thirty-four years. Together they had six children, who ranged in age from thirty-two to thirty-seven years.

At the time of the interviews, all six of Mrs Young's children lived at home. The house was a fairly large one by August Town standards and had five bedrooms. Mrs Young's husband worked as a maintenance man at the university and she was a dressmaker. She had been a dressmaker since the age of seventeen and had retired from full-time dressmaking at the age of fifty-one. She had found it too stressful and demanding, and at the time of the research continued to sew only for a few customers.

Of her six children, two daughters and four sons, three were unemployed, and the others, although employed, benefited from living at home, where they did not have to pay rent and contributed "what they could towards household expenses", said Mrs Young. They did not give a set amount regularly, as they were all marginally employed. Additionally, the two older sons had the obligation of children outside the home, and contributed financially to their children's upkeep.

Apart from her six children who lived with her, Mrs Young also had responsibility for two teenaged grandchildren, who also lived with her. These children, two girls, were the daughters of her two older sons. The mother of one had migrated to the United States when the child was two years old and Mrs Young's son had asked her to take care of the child. The other grandchild had lived with them since birth.

She said she had good relations with all her children, and the youngest, a son who had been unemployed for two years, was particularly helpful around the house. "He helps with the cooking, washes the dishes, does the shopping and helps with the cleaning of the house," she said.

There is evidence of the importance of children to women in Jamaica, and indeed the Caribbean. The traditionally high incidence of children born out of wedlock supports the assumption that, for the majority of women, motherhood is more important than wifehood. Whether or not women cared to admit that they saw children as an investment for the future, in 1990–91, having children who were helpful financially was a real advantage for those women who had them, as they would have been provided with another source to tap, not only in their old age but in the immediacy of the economic crisis. In 1990–91, pensions were unrelated to the cost of living, and women who thought they had saved enough to provide for themselves through their old age found that inflation in the economy had rendered their savings of much less value than they could possibly have imagined.

None of the middle-class women saw children as an investment for the future, but one (Respondent no. 154) had this to say about other groups of women: "The poor do not have children because they can afford them. They have children anyway. It is the only hope they have to ensure that they have enough children so some will help them in their old age." This middle-class woman believed that working-class women see their children as investments for the future. Another middle-class woman (Respondent no. 117) stated: "Children should never be seen as a guarantee for the future as they have their own lives to live and their own responsibilities. They might even migrate and you might never see them again. They might even stay in Jamaica and not help the parents, so the plan for children as insurance would not work, whereas if you had planned for yourself by having fewer children, it would be better." One working-class respondent (no. 17) remarked, "When I had my children I believed that as soon as they were able financially they would help me." This woman confirmed what the two middle-class women had argued: that working-class women see their children as investments for the future. Although this "investment" often does not pay off, my interviews with labour officials suggested that the state takes it into consideration and consequently regards itself as having no obligation to make realistic provision for such women. For example, one labour union worker said, "If the government was not aware that so many people have relatives abroad, who send the occasional barrel of clothing and other goods, maybe, just maybe, greater efforts would be made to ensure better social benefits for older persons."

Clearly, however, not all working-class women rely on their children as such investments. One is left to wonder about the variables within the working class that contribute to the differences in their views on the subject.

Although these women, in general, did not see children as insurance for the future, all but two of them had children. The women from the working-class community, however, had more children, a mean of 5.2 children, compared to the other women, who had a mean of 3.4 children. The difference in the number of children women in the two groups had speaks to the issues of different norms of family size in the two communities and the fact that during their child-bearing years, especially among the older women, those of the middle class would have had better access to family planning services.

It is my contention that women from midlife on managed their family and family life in such a way as to maximize opportunities for interdependence. An example of this might be seen in the fact that very few of the women lived alone. What real choices did such women have about their living arrangements and what advantage was it to them to share their house with other people? The data revealed that 53 per cent of the August Town women had adult offspring in their homes, as was the case for 55 per cent of the Hope Pastures women. Fifty-three per cent of the August Town women and 31 per cent of the Hope Pastures women had other people living in their homes, while 19 per cent and 14 per cent of the August Town and Hope Pastures women, respectively, lived alone.

Historically, working-class women, the group into which our August Town women would almost all have fallen, have always had family members living with them, hence this is the norm of family existence. For them, the situation has advantages in that resources can be shared and they need not be alone in their old age, but this reality also has negative consequences.[15] The negative is that women who must share their homes lose some of their independence and are at times burdened by the relatives who continue to live with them. For such women the "family home" is the place where all the offspring live, even when they begin their own families, and sometimes even after they are married. This, however, has not been the pattern for middle-class families. The fact that 55 per cent of our middle-class women had offspring living with them, while 31 per cent also had other relatives in residence, is an indication of some of the adjustments that were being made in terms of family life in relation to exorbitant rents and a generally high cost of living. The *Jamaica Survey of Living Conditions* (Statistical Institute of Jamaica 1989) provided some supporting evidence for small change in domestic arrangements for middle-class persons, where it showed an increase in the number of occupants of households over the years immediately before 1989.

The majority of the women in the study had their own homes and lived in them.[16] House ownership, power at the micro level, must be seen as a particularly valuable resource, which some of these women were able to use to their advantage in negotiation with their family members. The data show that where women were in a situation of house sharing, it was more likely that others shared with them than that they were in the reverse situation of being outside of their own home and sharing with others. The fact that most were in their own homes, and not in the homes of their offspring, indicates that those women were still in a positive negotiating position with their relatives, in a situation in which rental and mortgages would have been out of the reach of these relatives.[17]

It is much easier to remain relatively independent and in control of one's own affairs when one is in one's own home, although this was not always the case, as we see with Mrs Gooden (Case no. 9) in the next chapter. However, women who lived in their own homes were more likely to continue to be in house-sharing arrangements with their children and relatives, which were in some instances advantageous relationships where they could dictate the terms of the living arrangements. The following case is an example of such a situation.

Case No. 3

Mrs Nolan was sixty-three years old and a widow. She had worked as a teacher until her retirement three years previously. Her husband had also been a teacher and had been dead for two years.

She lived in a very well-appointed house in Hope Pastures. She had had no children of her own but had raised a niece and three other children from primary school age until they completed their secondary education.

Prior to her husband's death, the two of them lived alone. After her husband's death she asked her niece, who had serious financial problems, to come to live with her. Her niece had been a college student some years previously, and had dropped out of school after her marriage. She had had three children in quick succession and had been unable to keep up with her studies. The niece had recently gone back to college, and although her husband was employed as a trainee accountant, they were having difficulty paying their rent. Mrs Nolan therefore decided to invite her niece and family to share her house, rent-free.

The house was large enough, she said, for them not to get under one another's feet, and they had separate kitchens. "There is only one problem, but I'm getting used to it," she said. "The thing about it is that I used to love the quiet life, but now I have to get accustomed to a lot of noise in the house, from the children."

The advantage for Mrs Nolan would be that she no longer had to live on her own. It was not considered safe for a sixty-three-year-old woman to live alone in 1991.

A small number of women (eight women of the August Town sample and seven of the Hope Pastures sample) lived in the homes of their relatives. Those women were among the older women in the study and no longer worked outside their home. Some of the women who were still in their own homes expressed reservations about what would happen to them if the time should come when they needed to leave their current accommodation or dispose of it to cope with their living expenses in the event of "long life". They feared that because of the problems in the economy, problems of unemployment and inflation, their relatives would not be in a position to offer shelter or assistance to them. Those women actually made comments in the case studies that suggested that they were concerned about their future when they would no longer be economically independent.[18] They feared that their children would be unable to assist them to continue to live reasonably comfortable lives. In this regard, the following comment was fairly common: "I worry about the future sometimes, as life is so difficult economically, and the children have their own problems" (Respondent no. 117).

Other Children

The data from my survey show that 37 per cent of the working-class sample of women and 41 per cent of the other group of women had adopted or fostered children. Also, the two women in the study who had no natural children had adopted, fostered or "raised" children all of their adult years. The number of children adopted or fostered ranged from one to five, and the differences in pattern of adoption or fostering for the working-class and the middle-class women were not

Midlife and Older Women

statistically significant. This means that the women of both classes saw the need and took additional children into their homes.

Women take charge of children in order to help the children, because this is a common cultural expectation. This results in mutual benefits for children and older women in the long run, in most instances. None of the women gave this as their reason for deciding to take children into their care, but comments made casually in the case studies by some women about what they hoped such children might do for them, led me to the conclusion that women do indeed share the view expressed by the labour union official that children are a resource. For example, one middle-class woman said, "I'm glad that my daughter leaves her children here with me when she travels abroad, as without these grandchildren, it would just be me and [name of her husband] staring at one another. That would certainly not do."[19] A working-class woman said, "I'm glad I took my niece to live with me when she was twelve years old. Now she is older I have some one to get me a cup of tea when I'm not feeling so well."

Whatever might be the motivation for women to take children into their homes, there was no significant difference between the women of the middle class and working class in their desire to adopt or foster children. However, whereas among the working-class group the adopted child most often belonged to a daughter, son or niece, among the middle class, the child adopted or raised most likely belonged to a sister or a relative other than daughter or son. Daughters, sons and nieces of the working-class sample were more likely than the relatives of the middle-class group of women to be single persons who had started a family and, finding that they were unable to cope, needed someone to help with the children. Daughters, sons and nieces of the middle-class women were more likely to start their families with two parents, thus reducing the need to turn to their mothers to assist them in the child-rearing process. However, middle-class women did at times have responsibility for children of their sisters or other people, who might have gone abroad on study or other assignments. Apart from these children, whom women adopted and took charge of on a full-time basis, the women of this study also assisted their relatives in a number of ways, such as collecting children from school, and keeping children after school until their parents completed their workday. This was the situation for thirty-four women of each community.

FEELINGS OF CLOSENESS

Academic research (for example Massiah 1983 and Mohammed and Perkins 1999) supports the argument that women have a special relationship among themselves. Their respondents mainly cited female relatives and friends to whom they could turn when problems arose. In order to understand who were the family members to whom our women from midlife felt closest, and learn more about the persons to whom they were most likely to turn during periods of stress or difficulties, the issue of closeness was explored.

The women in the August Town sample felt closest first to their daughters, then to their mother or sister, then to their sons, then to their husbands. The Hope Pastures sample felt closest to their daughters, then to their mother or sister, then to their husbands, then to their sons. Some reported no preference and felt close to the entire family. Women from both classes felt closest to their daughters. Because marriage is an idealized state in the Caribbean, one would also expect that women should state that they felt close to their spouses, next in line to their daughters. This was the case for the middle-class women, who have already been shown to have more activities in common with their spouses, as well as being less independent from them.[20] However, August Town women stated their reality: that they felt closer to a number of people other than their husbands. For them reality did not conform to an idealized discourse of marriage.

The most important reasons given by the women for feeling closer to one relative over another were pragmatic on the whole. People said that they "got on well together", that "they had spent many years together" and "because they lived close by". Apart from the information available from the survey, the case studies also provided evidence that suggested that spatial or geographic closeness seemed to contribute to feelings of emotional closeness. Women were more likely to be close to relatives they saw frequently and those who lived nearby.

There appeared to be evidence of reciprocity between these women and their non-resident offspring as well as with those who were co-resident. They reported that such relatives provided some amount of financial assistance to them. It could be that the difficult economic situation pushed these women's offspring and other relatives emotionally closer to them, leading to a high level of cooperation and better opportunities to cope as a family. For example, Respondent no. 2 reported on the good relations she had with her children and the financial assistance she received from them. She stated, "I am only able to cope economically because of the support which I get from my two sons and my two daughters. They have always assisted me financially ever since they started to work. They give me enough to take care of my food, rent and the utilities [electricity, telephone and water]. Together they give me about J$2,000 per month.[21] They supply all my needs and I never have to request anything from them." She then added, "The reason why they respect me and treat me so good is that I educated them and brought them up in a way which enables them to survive in these difficult times." This, however, was the situation of this particular woman, but would not have been true for all others.

RELATIONS OF RECIPROCITY AT THE DOMESTIC LEVEL

It is assumed that one may learn about the nature of the day-to-day relationship that individuals have with other people by the acts of reciprocity involved in the relationship. If acts are performed one-sidedly, and if one party seems to be a burden on the relationship, then one might conclude that such a relationship is unequal or repressive. These women were asked about the tasks that they did around the home and the tasks that were done by others. Who does which particular tasks tells us about the nature of the relationship: who is being facilitated and who is being constrained. Already I had sought to analyse the power relations between women and their spouses as these relate to the sexual division of labour. I felt it was also necessary to look at what women did around the home in relation to other members of the family.

The most common things done by women of both groups for their relatives were what they referred to as the usual family caring (child-minding included), provision of shelter, housework and cooking. "Usual family caring" here refers to the provision of emotional support and to being available to listen and to give advice.

The women from the two groups, whether they worked outside the home or not, or whether they had part-time maids, as was often the situation with the Hope Pastures sample, did a variety of household tasks, such as washing, cooking, overseeing the housework and gardening. Many did all the housework (27 per cent of the working-class sample and 14 per cent of the middle-class sample). The differences in what they did were not statistically significant by class. Regardless of the class group to which they belonged, they did similar tasks, although the middle-class women who had maids would at times have some relief from the tasks they did. Some middle-class women now had to take on chores that they had relinquished two decades previously, because they could now only afford a "days worker" once or twice per week instead of a full-time worker.[22] A full-time helper was what they would have had in the past when domestic help had been less of a drain on the family's budget.

The other persons who performed tasks around the home were daughters, sons, husbands, as we saw earlier in the chapter, and grandchildren and nieces. The main tasks they did were what the women described as helping with the housework (25.7 per cent for the August Town sample and 12.3 per cent for the Hope Pastures sample) and odd jobs, such as shopping and paying bills. Sixty-one and seventy women of the working-class and middle-class samples, respectively, stated that relatives helped with household tasks. Among the August Town sample the ones most likely to help with the tasks were the daughters, then the husbands, then the sons. The daughters were twice as likely to help as were the sons. Among the middle-class group, it was the sons first, followed by the daughters, then the husbands who were most likely to help with the household tasks. This latter finding was an unexpected one, as it had been assumed that a daughter is more likely to help if she lives at home. The data reveal that in middle-class homes there were a total of twenty-eight sons and an equal number of daughters living at home with their mothers; the daughters and sons who were helping were not necessarily living in the same homes. The data suggest that the sons were more likely to be helpful around the home because they had no family living with them in their mothers' homes, while the daughters usually did. It might also be that the women were more likely to report that their sons were helpful around the home because whatever the daughters did was taken for granted, since daughters, as women, are expected to help, but they noticed more readily whatever the sons did for them, since sons do not traditionally help around the home.

The case studies revealed another role that women carried out in their families. They showed these women in a role that could be referred to as a "holding together" role. They were often the link, the bridge, between various members of the family, including members of different generations. They were the ones who ensured that letters were written to relatives abroad. They visited the sick in hospital. They were the link between their daughters and the fathers of their daughters' children, and their sons and the mothers of their sons' children, especially in the situation where these family members had not been married and where these relationships had fallen apart. They were sufficiently powerful to ensure that family members who would otherwise have drifted apart communicated with one another. This could be considered as part of the reproductive role of these women, in the sense that they contributed to the reproduction of the labour force and the stability of the family and extended family.

The case studies also showed these older women in what I would regard as a "representative role".[23] They were often called upon to represent others in situations where they were unable or unwilling to represent themselves, for example to attend health centres with ill children. This they did frequently, freeing their daughters and daughters-in-law from the responsibility and the problems associated with taking time off from work. They also attended parent-teacher meetings on behalf of these adult offspring in the representative role of "mother". In their representative role, they saw themselves as "the women in the middle", literally, in that they were called upon to fulfil various roles, for their own parents, as well as for people of their own generation and for their children.

FINANCIAL ASSISTANCE RECEIVED FROM RELATIVES

Financial assistance individuals receive from those around them speaks volumes about the nature of the relationship that is experienced. If we assume that possession of money and the ability to decide how and when to use it confers power, then we will be better placed to understand what was happening with midlife and older women and their relatives in this regard. It was not easy to discern exactly the nature of financial assistance received from relatives in this study. Demographers, as they conduct censuses, note that it is always difficult to obtain accurate information about people's financial situations. Clearly, for many women of the middle-class group, it was not necessary for them to receive any assistance. However, as many as 32 per cent of the August Town sample and 20 per cent of the Hope Pastures sample said they did receive financial assistance from relatives. The assistance was no great sum and was usually both irregular and very infrequent. Only 13 per cent of the August Town women and 5 per cent of the Hope Pastures women received this assistance on a monthly basis.

Sources of financial assistance included daughters, sons, spouses and other relatives. Only 3 per cent of the Hope Pastures women stated that they received financial assistance from their daughters, although in the case studies the women did make reference to financial assistance from more than three daughters. It would seem that this was less likely to be on a regular basis than such assistance from sons. Seventeen per cent of the August Town sample and 20 per cent of the Hope Pastures group reported receiving sums in excess of J$200 per month.

RELATIONSHIPS WITH OFFSPRING WHO LIVED ELSEWHERE

In order to understand more about the issues of power, independence and control in the lives of these older women, one needs to examine not only the relationships that they experienced with their relatives who lived with them, but also with their relatives who lived elsewhere. By good relations they meant visits and familial reciprocity from those who lived on the island and letters and gifts from those who lived abroad.

Most of these women reported good or very close relations between themselves and their children who lived elsewhere. More middle-class women reported good relations with their daughters, 94 per cent compared to 70 per cent for working-class women, and more middle-class women also reported better relations with sons than did the other group of women. This might relate to the marginally better economic situation of the women in the Hope Pastures sample, their ability to tap resources other than those of the family when in need, and their smaller numbers of children, which might reduce the general pressures of living in a society faced with numerous economic problems. It might also be that these mothers provided what they felt were normatively appropriate answers.

Women of both groups spoke of the importance of having a daughter and the data supported slightly better relations with daughters than with sons. Relations with nieces were also reported as being of great significance. More working-class mothers, however, reported relationships as "not good" with daughters and with sons than did the middle-class mothers. One gained the impression that family relations, where grown offspring were concerned, were better generally for the middle-class mothers. The explanation here might be that the offspring of these middle-class women were less likely to make demands on their mothers and so were less likely to be in conflict with them.

Relatives Abroad: Power Relations

In the same way that access to money could influence the relationships women had with local relatives, having relatives abroad, and whether these relatives provided financial assistance, was another way of understanding some aspects of family relations.

Many of the women in this study had relatives living abroad (58 per cent for the women in the August Town sample and 88 per cent for Hope Pastures) and, as a result of this, they were often required to take responsibility for these relatives' children. The higher percentage of relatives of the women in the Hope Pastures sample who were living abroad reflects the receiver countries' immigration bias, in that these countries prefer to accept skilled workers and workers with a high level of education, which would be the case of the relatives of the Hope Pastures women. The relatives abroad lived mainly in the United States, the United Kingdom and Canada and some respondents reported that they had two or three close relatives in those countries. The August Town women reported their relatives to be in service and in manual and clerical occupations, whereas the Hope Pastures women reported their relatives as being professionals. Many of these women with relatives abroad (50 per cent of the working-class group and 25 per cent of the middle-class group) received financial assistance from these relatives, but only 5 per cent said that they received this assistance regularly.

Although the August Town women had fewer relatives abroad, they reported a higher level of financial assistance from such relatives. This suggests that these relatives abroad felt more obliged to help their people at home than did the relatives of those in Hope Pastures. This obligation might relate to the fact that financial assistance had been given to them in terms of "passage" to get to these foreign countries and that the relatives at home continued to undertake responsibilities for them, for example the minding of children left behind.[24]

The importance of remittances from relatives abroad has been recognized by the Jamaican government and reference has already been made in chapter 1 to the impact this money has on the national economy.

Many of these women with relatives abroad (64 per cent of the August Town group and 100 per cent of the Hope Pastures group) stated that apart from financial assistance they also received gifts from their relatives.[25] The women of Hope Pastures referred to the "barrels" that were sent to them by their relatives.[26] Relatives also did other things for these women, such as provide accommodation when they travelled abroad (43 per cent for the August Town group and 7 per cent for Hope Pastures) and look after their children when such children were abroad working, studying or visiting. These women also reported that their relatives bought "spare parts" for them abroad.[27] That a higher percentage of the August Town women's relatives accommodated them and helped their children when they were abroad might be an indication of a continuation of "community" and extended family, which is generally accepted as more prevalent among lower-income persons. Additionally, the lower percentage among the Hope Pastures women might mean that these persons preferred to make their own arrangements and that they had persons other than family, such as business colleagues and friends, who would help to arrange their accommodation when they were abroad.[28]

With reference to familial obligations, the ones the women reported as having for their relatives abroad were financial dealings, minding children (see, for example, Case no. 4 below), and sending local food. A total of fifty-three women (17 per cent of the August Town sample and 36 per cent of the Hope Pastures sample) stated that they "did things" for relatives abroad, although some were hard put to state what some of these "things" were. A total of eighty-seven women from the two communities stated that they did nothing for relatives abroad.[29]

We note that middle-class women who helped relatives abroad undertook more financial dealings for their relatives, while working-class women were more likely to mind children (58.8 per cent versus 8.1 per cent). What this means is that women of both groups were prepared to help their relations in the ways in which they were best able, and in ways that have been typical for the particular group. The case below illustrates this.

Case No. 4

Miss Norma was fifty-three years old. She worked as a domestic helper and lived in August Town. She was a single woman who had had one child when she was sixteen years old. This child, a son, was thirty-seven years old at the time of the interviews. Miss Norma had full-time responsibility for her son's three children; boys aged sixteen, fifteen and thirteen years. The children lived with her in her three-room house, and she treated them as her own. Her son had left the children with her seven years previously when he migrated to the United States. He had earlier separated from their mother with whom he had had a common-law relationship. He took the children from her because he felt that his mother would be better able to take care of his children.

Miss Norma stated that her son did not send her enough money for the children. The money was not sent regularly and often had to be requested. Consequently she struggled, she said, with her own income to keep the children in high school. Indeed, it was some achievement that she had been able to get them into high school at all, as in Jamaica in 1991, in order to accomplish this for any child, the child needed to take private tuition and then the Common Entrance Examination. These private lessons had to be paid for and often represent a sizeable proportion of the low-income family's budget.

Miss Norma saved her money in a "partner" and in a burial scheme. Besides her regular job which she did four days each week, she frequently cooked fish and baked pastries at her home to supplement her income of J\$560 per month. She sold these items in her landlord's shop at the front of the yard.

The children she said had "healthy appetites" and she had to ensure that they did not eat all the food before the end of the week. She said: "With my small salary of J\$560 per month, so many times we have to do without."

Miss Norma, now beyond the child-bearing years, said, "Sometimes I am sorry that I did not have a few more children, even three, especially a girl. It is a good thing to have a daughter." Miss Norma was asked what was special about having a daughter. She stated that "it was a good thing to have a daughter, as daughters are more dependable than sons in your old age".

ON BEING OLDER

In order to explore the issue of ageism (that is the prejudices and stereotypes that are applied to older people on the basis of their age) and power within the context of the family and the household, women from midlife on were asked what it meant to them to be older members of their families and households. By and large, the experience of ageing brought more rewards to the women of the working-class community than to the Hope Pastures women.

The responses were varied but it is of interest to note that the majority said that being older in the family had no special meaning. Another noteworthy response on being older in the family was that it meant "more stress and more work". This was mentioned by 6 per cent and 12 per cent of the August Town and Hope Pastures samples, respectively. The higher percentage of Hope Pastures women who reported "more stress" would have been a reflection of the "changing economy" and of the unaccustomed pressures that were being placed on middle-class women as they sought to organize their families. This certainly was a very important response. To be older was not to be able to relax and take it easier. Being older for some brought a degree of disappointment in that they had to continue in paid employment when they would rather have retired. For some, it was also stressful as a result of the contradiction some experienced between expectation and reality in relation to family and state obligations.

"More respect" was mentioned by a higher percentage of the working-class women, 16 per cent compared to 2 per cent for the other community, which suggests that working-class women actually perceived that they are shown more respect as they grow older. The question that has to be asked then is: "Why this apparent difference in the age at which respect is shown, and what is it that causes offspring and relatives to show respect?" Given that unmarried motherhood has until relatively recently been stigmatized in Jamaica,[30] respect is only shown when the woman to be respected has proven herself to be deserving in ways other than those related to her marital circumstances and family situation. It could be that this respect only comes to them when such women have acquired some material substance and proven themselves as providers; when they have married or given up living in a common-law relationship. When they grow older and acquire some of the trappings of so-called respectable living, when they have resources of time and money to become more prominent or influential in their own communities, only then will those around them actually feel proud of them and show them respect. Some of this might be interpreted as people's response to older women's multiple identities, which cause people to relate to them, not only as older women, but as women of a particular class or as women with particular responsibilities within the community.

CONTROLLING OLDER WOMEN

Control and Independence

Past research has shown that in Jamaica and the rest of the Caribbean, women become more independent and self-assured as they grow older (Durant-Gonzalez 1980; Momsen 1989; Mohammed and Perkins 1999) and are then better able to make decisions about their lives and about the use of the resources available to them. What one hears in daily conversation within the culture also suggests that this is the case, and that older women are generally respected within their own class situation and community context. However, older women in some situations find that they cannot be as independent as they would like to be and, indeed, that certain controls are being placed on their lives.

Some of the women whom this researcher got to know better, as a result of the case studies, presented themselves as independent women who made important decisions when they wanted to. They also spoke in a manner that suggested that they knew, within certain limits, what was best for themselves and their families. However, they added that whenever these decisions had to be taken, they consulted with family members. They were unanimous in that, if the relatives disagreed with their particular decisions, they would usually reconsider and quite likely not act. Only 5 per cent of the working-class women and 15 per cent of the middle-class women stated that they would proceed with their intended action if their relatives disagreed with their judgment. This information, perhaps more than anything else we have seen so far, tells us something very definite about the power relations between women and their relatives. This says that most women were reluctant to go against the wishes of their relatives and that this was truer for working-class women than for women of the middle class. Although the women presented themselves as fairly independent, very few were prepared to make important decisions without consultation, and having made those decisions were willing to renege on them if they felt they would not have support from relatives. The question that is then raised is: what was it that gave those relatives the power to influence such women?

Why Relatives Had Influence

The data collected revealed that both middle-class and working-class women had similar responses with regard to the reasons they were likely to be influenced by relatives. The reasons given were, for example, that the relatives made wise decisions, that they had confidence in such relatives, that they were "very close", and that the relatives had their best interests at heart. The responses suggest that those women were influenced by relatives on whom they were emotionally dependent. Those closest to the individual were most influential. It would seem also that those women were reluctant to disrupt existing social relations with their relatives in their bid to make forceful new decisions. There were also financial considerations where influence was concerned, and it was clear that, in some instances, access to money meant "power".

We see then that closeness was a factor that influenced power relations in the family, causing relatives to behave other than they might have done in the absence of such closeness. Some of the working-class women said that they were influenced because they needed the person's financial assistance. Thus, it was shown that control could be exercised over the individual because of financial dependence. The data revealed that this was more likely to be the case for the women of the working-class community. Presumably, though, middle-class women were not immune to influence in this regard. And given the economic problems encountered by families in 1990–91, it could be expected that, at the national level, more middle-class women might have had to negotiate for financial assistance for themselves, bargaining with other resources that they possessed, given their changed economic fortunes.

Most of those women who were still in intimate relationships presented a picture of being at ease with themselves in their relationships. They had, over time, determined what gave them power and what they needed to do to keep outside of the influence of some of their relatives; in other words, how to guard their relative independence. Only two women spoke of overtly conflict-filled situations that existed between themselves and their spouses. The absence of discussion on the matter does not negate the existence of such relationships but suggests that these women's behaviour was in keeping with the cultural expectations of what Caribbean male-female behaviour should be for this age group. The norm is that men can do "whatever" and women are expected to forgive them.[31]

Sexuality: Reassertion of Male Control

The issue of sexuality is mentioned here in the context of family, as these women's sexuality was intricately bound up with their relationship with their children. This was especially the case for those women who were widowed or separated from their spouses. Sexuality for most of these women was mainly about "sex", that is active sexual intercourse, and feeling good about themselves as sexual beings. However, for others it also included "feelings of intimacy", which they talked about, but which did not have to manifest itself in acts of sexual intercourse.

Sexuality, when it concerns women fifty years old and over, can evoke emotive feelings because of the ambivalence in the discourse on the sexuality of women beyond the child-bearing age. (This is developed further in chapter 5.) The case studies revealed that some women deliberately subdued, or kept secret, various aspects of their sexuality because of their fear of being in conflict with their grown offspring. However, most of these women felt reasonably comfortable discussing issues of sexuality such as society's views on what should be the sexual attitude of women of their age group, the women's own views on their attitude towards sex and the over-fifties, and comments on their own sexual activity or its absence. Their views on society's attitude to their expression of their sexuality were mixed, with some stating that society sought to control this expression, while others said that society did not care about how older people expressed their sexuality.

As I had anticipated, a few women were not comfortable discussing the most intimate aspects of their sexuality, such as whether or not they were sexually active. However, almost equal numbers from both groups, 82 per cent of the working class and 88 per cent of the middle class, did speak frankly about this aspect of their lives. Those who were sexually active included women across the entire age range in this research.[32] These were almost equally distributed across the two class groups.[33] Those sexually active were mainly the younger women, fifty to fifty-nine years old, but women at seventy years old were also sexually active among the middle class.

What women said and did with regard to their sexuality was obviously bound up with ideas about what was the proper personal and sexual behaviour for women of this age group. The working-class women tended to be more restrained in their responses in relation to the sexuality of older women. Those women also tended to be more overtly religious, and belonged to the evangelical denominations, which led me to seek for a positive correlation between religion and the attitudes of so-called older women toward their sexuality.

However, it was not only religion that appeared to constrain women in their attitudes toward their sexuality and in their related behaviour. The data revealed that some women gave very careful thought to their behaviour. For example, some stated that they were cautious not to behave in ways that might be interpreted as "wanting to look younger than their years". Others were reluctant to accept male companionship, or establish new relationships, because they were concerned about what their sons, especially, might think of them. This suggests that sons, more so than other relatives, had the ability to influence women's behaviour in relation to their sexuality. This was more likely to be the case for working-class women but was not exclusively so, as a smaller group of middle-class women also made reference to not wanting to offend their sons and other relatives by establishing new, intimate friendships in their older years. This also was more likely to be the situation for women who were over sixty years old, which suggests that those women who were fifty to fifty-nine years old, the midlife women, and who might have been in the situation of wanting to become involved in new relationships were less likely to experience controlling influence from their relatives. Those relatives did not seem to see such women as "old" and without "personal" needs, as they did the older group of women.

Not only did the working-class women appear to have aspects of their sexuality externally controlled because of their religiosity and their relationship with their sons, but the data showed that they were convinced that this was what was expected of them. They were much more likely than the middle-class women to feel the need to conform to what was expected.[34] The data showed that the women of the working-class community were more inclined to believe that society did not expect women of this age group to be sexually active. In the absence of an alternate discourse about their sexuality, and given whatever power was available to them, older women, especially older working-class women, were fully controlled in the area of their sexuality.

There was no doubt that many of the women of the two communities had a good sense of themselves as sexual beings. Some reported on the advances that were made frequently to them by men of all ages, young men included. However, more importantly, the data portrayed these women as having a sense of independence as to how they preferred to lead their lives. For example, most of those who were no longer married said they were quite happy to live without a male partner. The women interviewed here were almost all deeply religious, and one might be tempted to conclude that those who had the opportunity, but rejected sexual activity, were able to put issues of sexuality out of their minds in many instances or give it a low priority by concentrating much of their energies on service to church, family and community.

CONCLUSION

These women played numerous roles within their families and interacted in a variety of relationships with them. They generally managed to balance the power relations between themselves and their spouses to ensure the relatively smooth functioning of their households. They were still actively mothering offspring who should long have left home. They also performed active roles as grandmothers to children who lived with them permanently and to children who stayed with them periodically. They were also workers for an income and they played the role of factotum to the family.

Although some of these women were in dire economic straits, the data revealed that they were available, although not always willing, to participate in activities that would be of assistance to their immediate and extended families. Some grandmothers were very resistant to participating in the traditional grandmothering roles, such as free child-minding and grocery shopping for their daughters, because they were too busy themselves in paid employment. This says something about a relatively new set of power relations that have been established between mothers and their offspring in recent years. This may be seen as their resistance to the role of caregiver first and foremost, which has been allocated to them in the dominant discourse. As older women become more involved in paid activity outside the home, they see themselves as less dependent on relatives and make themselves less readily available to be "used" by some relatives who would do so. Nonetheless there was no denying that family was of tremendous importance to these women. They were there for their families and at times even inconvenienced themselves while they sought to assist and occasionally indulge their various family members even in situations of relatively scarce resources.[35]

The various roles of Caribbean women, as mothers, workers and wives, have been well documented (Roberts and Sinclair 1978; Massiah 1983; Powell 1984; Mohammed and Perkins 1999) but one would expect that there would be significant changes in these roles as women aged. The results of this study suggest that for many women these roles did not change significantly once they started to undertake responsibilities for their adult offspring, and women from midlife on continued in the roles they had taken on in their late thirties and forties and added more caring roles as they matured.[36] Whatever had been expected of them in the past, in their earlier familial roles, would continue to be expected of them and would only change if they became ill or incapacitated. In this study only about ten of the two hundred women would have been seen as too ill to continue to play the traditional roles to their families and households. Consequently, most of them were still involved in roles that they would have had since the time they became responsible mothers. These roles were executed, maybe not with the same intensity and absorption as in earlier years, but certainly some still had roles, which, from their comments, it would seem that they had expected to relinquish when they became older or when their offspring had grown.

The data gathered reflected a gendered division of labour even within the home. These women reported that there were tasks that they were unable to convince their spouses to do. Not only were they unable to convince them, but the women appeared to take the division for granted and the tasks they had to do as inevitably theirs.

As discussed in chapter 1, there were tremendous changes in the Jamaican economy in the late 1980s and into 1990–91, which adversely affected these women and their families. The women, though, despite the economic pressures that threatened to engulf them and the need to relinquish lifestyles that had been more advantageous to them, conducted their lives in ways that made the best use of the resources available to them. They were very conscious of the relationships in which they were involved with their family and community, even if they would not have described these as power relations, for example, whether or not they minded children for their relatives or allowed them to share their homes. They knew to whom they could turn when they were in need, and they also knew who depended on them, and what had to be done about those relationships, even if they were not always able to effect the solutions they had in mind. In all of this, though, they realized that despite all the "work" they did, their family, community and the government did not always support their efforts, leaving them at times short of or without the resources to do the tasks that they realized had to be done, which often had been imposed on them by relatives and by the inadequacies of state provisions.

Nevertheless, these women were almost all constantly trying to work out coping strategies that would assist them and their families, sometimes in close consultation with family members living abroad. What was really striking about the women of the two communities was that they did not appear daunted by the changing fortunes of the Jamaican economy, which had negatively impacted them and their relatives, leaving many unemployed and underemployed, while they faced increased costs all around. Those women continued to give of themselves in ways that Jamaican families have always expected of women of this age group, whether or not they were supported by family, community or state.

What was particularly interesting about family relations was that there were not nearly as many differences as there were similarities by class for these women. Middle-class women as well as working-class women accepted the dominant discourse's portrayal of them as caregivers, and women in both groups did their share of caregiving. In both communities, similar percentages of women had adult off-spring sharing their homes with them, were heads of household and adopted and fostered children. And in like numbers they expressed appreciation for having had daughters. They were also influenced by relatives for very similar reasons when they had to make important decisions. It was in relation to the issue of "close-ness" that we saw a real difference in the responses of these two groups of women. Middle-class women favoured the expected "closeness" between man and wife in a way in which working-class women did not.

Much of what women of this age group did was in response to a combination of factors, including the type of interaction that they experienced with their daughters, sons, husbands and the wider society, and the absence of any discourse about "midlife and older women" that constituted any existence for them other than as caregivers or, in extreme old age, dependent. Women helped their daughters, even when to do so was burdensome. Caring was a normative expectation, but might be understood also as, "I'll help you now, using the power available to me – house, money, time, etc."; in other words, such care was a response to daily realities. Additionally, women helping their daughters and grandchildren provided them with opportunities for building emotional ties and feelings of closeness, which were very important to these women. Women of the working class especially were much more inclined to feel closer to their blood relatives than conjugal relatives. Similar findings were noted by Smith (1982). Another area in which discursive power worked against these women was most definitely in the area of sexuality. Women did not always do what they wanted to do sexually because they were reluctant to offend their sons and their community members even if they were receiving no financial help from them. Their alternate discourses of sexuality were repressed or silent; consequently they were controlled by the existing discourses of the sexuality of older women.

Finally, a discourse does exist that portrays women from midlife on in the caring role, which most often they are, whether or not they wanted it. But the daily realities demanded that they adopted a providing role too, while at the same time hoping that their relatives, if not the state, would increase the support, financial, material and physical, required to enable them to more efficiently carry out their caring roles.

CHAPTER 3
WORK AND THE MIDLIFE AND OLDER WOMAN

A friend of mine goes abroad and buys clothes and shoes and I walk around and sell them. Every day as I walk about in the hot sun, I'm feeling much older. I was born in 1927 and had six children. I'm not young anymore, but I need to keep working.
— *Interview with Respondent no. 27*

I don't think that I have come upon any discrimination because of my age but there are some things which older women face. Some employers are not kind to older women. Where older women are capable and have a commitment to the work, they end up having to do more than their fair share.
— *Interview with Respondent no. 154*

INTRODUCTION

This chapter explores the issue of work in the life of midlife and older women in Jamaica, noting the power relations that influence their lives at work as they interact with family and community in matters relating to their work in and outside the home. It argues that the dominant societal discourses surrounding work in the lives of midlife and older women do not show them as being nearly as resourceful as they really are and only grudgingly acknowledge their contribution. Additionally it is generally accepted in the society that older women are "taken care of" by the family and so do not need to have lucrative jobs because their needs are supposedly met.

This chapter shows some degree of similarity in the lives of the two groups of women, in that they almost all "worked", although some did not themselves see much of what they did as work because the society undervalues what they do. The chapter argues also that these women were able and willing to participate more fully in the paid workforce, but that the opportunities for such employment were limited, especially for working-class women.

The chapter is organized into three main sections and a number of subsections. The first section provides a brief historical background on women and work in Jamaica. The second looks specifically at what midlife and older women do, drawing on the data from the survey and the case studies. The final section draws some conclusions about power and work in the lives of women of the age group under discussion.

WOMEN AND WORK IN JAMAICA: A BRIEF OVERVIEW

Historical Background

The issue of work in the lives of Jamaican women who are midlife and older has already been raised in the introduction. Table 1 shows that large numbers of women of this age group worked outside the home as well as in the home. The tradition of women working is not new; women have always worked, from the earliest historical period. Mathurin (1975) documents the work that women did during the period of slavery, which was determined primarily by race. Black women did a variety of jobs, including manual work in the fields along with men. Some also worked as house servants in the master's home. Coloured women, more frequently than black women, worked as house servants, while white women supervised their maids within the home.

Nowadays, what women do in Jamaica is most often determined by their educational level and class position, enabling them to be in a variety of occupations especially if they are middle class. This was not always the case, however, as in order to be able to take advantage of the available jobs in the society, women first needed to have a certain level of education that was not always available to them. Miller (1986, 26) notes that, "During the post emancipation period 1834 to 1865 in Jamaica, the institutional structure of education reflected the plural nature of the society. Only elementary education was offered in the colony. All parents paid fees for their children."[1] Because fees had to be paid, girls often did not benefit from education in this early period, as preference was given to male children by the parents.[2] With reference to this preference given to boys in the post-emancipation communities, Miller (1986, 27) writes: "It could be that these communities, motivated as they were by the expectation of a new life and society, sought and gave opportunities to boys following the sexist tradition of that era. The British tradition to that point, and certainly in the Victorian era, was decidedly patriarchal." Miller (1986, 27) also notes that "most of the West African tribes that came to Jamaica – Ibo, Dahomeian, Yoruba and Congo were patrilineal and patriarchal",[3] and that "the possibilities exist that despite the influences of creolization and slavery, the Blacks after emancipation sought opportunities for the advancement of their sons more than for their daughters in keeping with their African ancestry".

Johnson (1986), Lobell (1986) and Standing (1981) track the employment opportunities available to women in Jamaica since the turn of the twentieth century and argue that women who worked outside the home were much more likely to be domestic workers and servants than to be engaged in any other kind of work. Domestic service has been a prevalent form of female employment in Jamaica since the beginning of the twentieth century and throughout it, running second only to agriculture (Johnson 1986, 4), in which rural women continue to be heavily involved. So important was this type of job to what was expected of women that at the turn of the century there were domestic schools, which prepared women for such work.

Domestic service was then, and still is, an area that provides low wages, but attracts large numbers because women are unable to find anything else to do. With regard to wages, Johnson (1986, 26) wrote:

> In absolute terms and certainly relative to other labourers, the domestic's wage over time has not improved very much. In 1920 the domestic wage was poised between the agricultural labourer whose wages she bettered but below the labourer in trade and manufacture. By 1925 the domestic wage situation had slipped below everyone else's.

The *Blue Book of Jamaica* (1945) notes that not only were domestics being paid less, but they were working at least twenty hours more than any other category of worker.

In later years though, women were able to participate more fully in the education process and were able to train as nurses and teachers, which were the first major professional areas for women.[4] In more recent times, especially in the last sixty years, women have taken advantage of whatever opportunities have presented themselves. But despite these opportunities, until the 1940s, women, especially those of the working class, continued to work within a relatively narrow band of employment opportunities.

Johnson (1986) notes that by 1955, women were beginning to turn away from service. Their desire to try to find something other than domestic service to do is reflected in M.G. Smith's 1974 study, which makes reference to occupational choices in rural Jamaica. In that study, girls ten to fifteen years old who were interviewed in 1955 were least likely to choose domestic service as a future occupation. But although younger women in 1955 did not want to go into domestic service, in reality many of the lower socio-economic group found nothing else to do. This was the case because the educational system did not provide more than a small number of them with the educational tools required for them to find alternate employment.

What would have been the source of employment for middle-class women? Those who sought to be employed would have worked as clerks, nurses, teachers, and postal service workers. What is also interesting about this period and the employment of women is that those women who chose to become career women within the civil service would not have been able to marry, and if after securing such employment they chose to marry, they would have been forced to resign from their jobs.[5]

It might be instructive to note some of the developments that actually took place in terms of women's employment after the 1940s. During the post–World War II period, women were steadily incorporated into the workforce. Women more than doubled their numbers in the classifiable labour force between 1943 and 1984, changing the sex ratio in the labour force from 36 per cent for women in 1943 to 45 per cent in 1985 (Gordon 1987) and from a situation in 1943 when a little more than a third of all working women were domestics to there being 16 per cent in that category of worker in 1984.

In more recent times, the situation has improved marginally for working-class women; with the industrialization of the 1960s and the 1970s, more of these women were able to move into other areas of employment, and in the 1980s women were employed in the free zones, in garment manufacturing and data entry operations. These jobs gave women some independence but did not move them out of low status, low-wage employment. Additionally, the factories located in the free zones of that period preferred to employ younger women. We note, though, the continued importance of domestic work, as shown by Anderson (1989) who reports that 70 per cent of domestic workers interviewed did this type of work because it was the only job available to them.

Although there have been wide swings in the economy over the years, female labour-force participation levels have remained very high despite high levels of unemployment throughout the twentieth century (Standing 1981; Gordon 1987; Planning Institute of Jamaica 2002).[6] This continued high level of female participation is referred to also by Deere (1990), who argues that the labour-force participation rate for female heads of household in Kingston is high, being 82 per cent and not far below the level of 92 per cent for male heads of household. This is important for this study, as 43 and 45 per cent of the women interviewed in August Town and Hope Pastures, respectively, were heads of households and 58 per cent and 70 per cent were in paid employment. This representation, although for a "community", was quite similar to that which Gordon (1987) found for the Jamaican labour force as a whole. He noted that women make up half of the labour force and that most of these women were employed full-time.[7] In 2002, female participation levels in the labour force continued to increase and did so by 1.8 per cent over the previous year to 55.4 per cent of the labour force (Planning Institute of Jamaica 2002).

The Labour Force

Jamaica had a population of 2.5 million in 1990.[8] The labour force of persons over fourteen years old was 1,060,100 in October 1990, as is shown in Table 1. Of these, 493,100 were female and 567,000 were males, and approximately 123,000 were women forty-five years and over. The unemployment rate for women in 1989 was twice that for men: 26.1 per cent versus 10.9 per cent (Planning Institute of Jamaica 1990).[9] Below, we see something of the employment structure as it was during the period of this research. Table 1 shows that women were well represented in the labour force across all age groups and we are able to note the number of midlife and older women who are officially part of that labour force. Large numbers of those who were employed in the informal economy would not have been represented here, and those who take care of children and the elderly, family and non-family, might also not have been represented.

With regard to women and work in the Caribbean, Deere (1990, 61) noted at the time:

> The growing number of women in the labour force may appear contradictory in view of increased unemployment and underemployment in the Caribbean generally. However women are forced into the labour market precisely because of increased unemployment among men and because real wages of employed household members are decreasing, contributing to an overall reduction in household income. Women are able to find jobs even when men are not, because they work for lower wages, because the labour market in the Caribbean (as elsewhere) is highly segregated by gender, and because a high percentage of women work in the informal sector.

Although this did not relate specifically to older women, much of what was said is directly relevant to the situation of such women in Jamaica. A larger number of the survey sample than I had anticipated were at work in 1990–91: 34 per cent and 54 per cent of the August Town and Hope Pastures women, respectively, worked in the formal sector and 24 per cent and 2 per cent, respectively, of the two groups worked in the informal sector.[10] Many needed to be at work because their menfolk, spouses and adult male offspring, were unemployed. It was easier for women to find employment, which was quite often short-term in nature, because women, more than men, were prepared to work for minimal wages or become involved in informal sector activities. The case studies demonstrated these types of income-earning activities. Case no. 5,

TABLE 1

Total Labour Force by Age (October 1990)

Age	Female		Male	
(years)	No.	%	No.	%
14–19	46,400	9.4	68,300	12.0
20–24	96,400	19.4	102,200	18.0
25–34	131,300	26.6	138,700	24.5
35–44	89,200	18.1	93,900	16.6
45–54	67,700	13.7	72,900	12.9
55–64	40,900	8.3	51,200	9.0
65 +	21,200	4.2	39,800	7.0
Total	493,100	100.0	567,000	100.0

Source: Statistical Institute of Jamaica 1990, 9.

which is reported on later in this chapter, shows Respondent no. 27 earning a fairly large income (J$2,000 or US$200) per month,[11] by walking through numerous communities selling clothes and shoes imported from the United States, to ensure a better standard of living for herself, her husband, her two adult offspring at home (the male being unemployed), and two grandchildren.[12]

WORK AND THE WOMEN OF AUGUST TOWN AND HOPE PASTURES

Differences and Similarities

The women of August Town were engaged in some instances in work that was very different from work done by the women of Hope Pastures, while in other instances their work was similar. For example, women who gave their occupation as housewife would have had some similarities in terms of how they spent their days, but there would also have been some differences, as almost all the women of Hope Pastures had domestic help to assist them with their household chores.

One aspect of work in which similarities between the two communities was found was in the area of childminding. In keeping with the expectations of what family life should be like in the Caribbean, older women helped out with the children of their relatives and of the community. Affirmation of this expectation was found in August Town as well as in Hope Pastures.

Another similarity in the type of activity in which women became involved was that women from both groups took boarders into their homes or, more frequently, rented a part of their home. This was one way in which women were able to increase their income. It was easier for Hope Pastures women to do this because they had larger homes, and because their own offspring were more likely to have moved into their own homes, leaving vacant rooms available for potential boarders or tenants. Nonetheless, some women of August Town, usually those with better than average homes, were also able to attract tenants or boarders to their homes. In both situations, student-tenants and occasionally boarders from the nearby University of the West Indies and the College of Arts, Science and Technology (now renamed the University of Technology) were to be found.

Another way in which the lives of those two sets of women were similar was that they almost all "worked". That is they were almost all in paid or unpaid work. Only those few who were actually in poor health had no "work" to do as such. They worked as housewives and in and out of the home in a wide range of activities.

Midlife and Older Women

They were remunerated differently, however, in that Hope Pastures women tended to be relatively better paid, as we will see in the section that follows. The August Town women were less well paid and worked mainly in the informal sector. Their ability to improve their income depended on whether or not they were able to secure additional jobs or additional hours of work within the situation in which they were already employed.

If we refer to the introduction, in which the two communities of August Town and Hope Pastures are described, we will understand in another sense some of the reasons work was different in the lives of those two groups of women. August Town was a mixed community, in the sense that it housed residences as well as commercial operations. Some of the August Town women who worked outside the home actually worked within their community. Hope Pastures, conversely, in 1990–91 was a residential community with no commercial operations therein. Consequently, women who worked out of the home worked outside the community. This required that Hope Pastures women organized for work differently in that they needed some form of transport to get them to work. They would also not be able to get back home readily during the course of the work day.

Women as Productive Workers

It was clear from the survey that, whatever might have been the common societal understanding about the work and life habits of women from midlife on, work was important in their lives. This could be seen from the fact that 128 (64 per cent) of those women earned an income, either outside the home or within the home. Of these women, fifty-eight were from August Town and seventy were from Hope Pastures.

The August Town women were involved in twenty-five main occupations.[13] These included cleaning, domestic work, vending and other selling jobs, and dressmaking. For these women, the categories of traders, unskilled manual and household helpers or domestics represented 59 per cent of recent employment for those no longer in the paid labour force. Domestic service alone represented 25 per cent. The Hope Pastures women had a wider range of occupations (forty-three), which included teaching, nursing, real estate, accounting, law, personnel, senior administration and medicine.[14] Three women had doctorates and a great deal of responsibility in their jobs. The important categories for the Hope Pastures women's current occupation were lower level managerial (27 per cent); lower-level technical and supervisory (25 per cent); high-level managerial and professional, such as top-level civil servants and university lecturers (18 per cent) and housewives (15 per cent). The differences here were statistically highly significant.

Although there were fewer spouses than women, the spouses of the working-class women were involved in thirty-four different occupations and the middle-class women's spouses were involved in forty-nine. This indicates that men had a wider range of employment options.

It was not only the fifty- to fifty-nine-year-olds who were involved in the paid labour force, but also the older women. The data show that most of the women in paid employment out of the home were those aged fifty to fifty-nine years, but thirty-seven of those who worked for wages out the home were between sixty and seventy-four. Seven of these women had actually retired from the formal labour force but had returned to work or had been asked to continue working after formal retirement.

Of these women in paid employment, thirty-eight of the August Town and fifty-four of the Hope Pastures women reported that they contributed a significant portion of their income to their families. They reported that food and general household expenses were the main areas into which they placed their income. This was the case for 73 per cent of the August Town women and 72 per cent of the Hope Pastures women.

All but one of the August Town women who reported themselves as currently employed for an income worked full-time. This was also the case for fifty of the Hope Pastures women who were currently working for pay. (This included people who had retired and gone back to work.)

The women of Hope Pastures complained bitterly about their incomes, given the already high and constantly increasing cost of living. However, they were less reluctant to state exactly how much money they received than were the women of August Town. Not all the respondents who worked for an income provided information about their income. Of the 120 who stated that they worked for an income, only thirty-four working-class women and thirty-two middle-class women gave details of their income.

The wages reported for August Town women were low in relation to the cost of living and salaries earned by other groups.[15] In 1991, the income required for the basic food basket was J$828.16 per month. Fifty-two per cent of the August

Town women who were working for wages earned less than this each month. The maximum for this group was J$2,000, which only three of the August Town women earned per month. For the two groups together, wages ranged from J$460 per month, which was earned by one domestic helper, to J$20,000 per month, which was earned by one medical doctor. The mean income for the sixty-six women who answered the relevant questions was J$919 for August Town and J$5,727 for Hope Pastures.[16]

Generally salaries were low and the differential between the mean incomes of the women of August Town and Hope Pastures was not that great because the higher incomes of a small number of middle-income women had skewed the income distribution pattern. Had the incomes of these women been removed prior to the calculation of the mean salaries, the reality would be that all had relatively low incomes, which placed them at a disadvantage in a society with a rapidly increasing cost of living.

Education and Work Opportunities

More of the Hope Pasture women, the women from the middle-class community, were able to find employment in the formal sector because of the privileged position that they had in the society, as a result of their higher levels of education. The Hope Pastures women worked in the civil service and had jobs in which they could be employed until they reached the formal retirement age, sixty years. However, some, having retired, were re-employed – this was the case for seven of the Hope Pastures women.

The survey data also revealed that although 74 per cent of the working-class women had attended primary school, only 57 per cent had completed their primary education and received at least seven years of such education. Conversely, all the middle-class women had completed their primary education. In addition to primary education, 7 per cent of the working-class women had received some additional special educational training. Among the middle-class women, 9 per cent had graduated from nursing school; 11 per cent from teachers' college; 16 per cent had bachelor's degrees and 14 per cent had higher degrees. The difference in the educational experiences of the two groups was statistically highly significant.

Reasons for Working

Why did women of this age group work for an income? There were at least three reasons: (1) that the economy needed their skills; (2) that their personal economic situations rendered their continued involvement in the labour force a necessity; and (3) that they wished to serve the community. These explanations were relevant to the situation of most of those women who worked for an income. Middle-class women who had retired were recalled or kept on the job after retirement because of the skills they possessed. Also the inflationary trend in Jamaica at the time caused some who wished to retire from paid employment to continue to work. This was true in both class groups.

Women worked in and outside the home because they were caught up in family situations in which they felt they had no choice but to provide both income and care to children, grandchildren, spouses, and a small number of "adopted" dependents. Women also worked because some genuinely wanted to do so. For some, however, their work situation was a response to the stark reality of their lives, which included factors such as not having savings, not having children able to help them financially, and that the need to continue to prepare for their future dictated this.

One frequently mentioned reason for working, especially among the working class, was that the other members of the family were unable to find employment. Such was the case of Mrs Smith of August Town, which follows.

Case No. 5

Mrs Smith was sixty-four years old and married. She was the mother of seven children: two daughters and five sons, ranging in age from twenty to thirty-one years. She received very little education (three years of schooling) as a child and said she felt badly about it. She described herself as "in fairly good health and only suffering from arthritis and poor vision, headache and dizziness".

She had lived with her husband for thirty-three years and had been legally married for thirteen years of that time. Mr Smith had been employed with the Jamaica Omnibus Service (JOS), but was made redundant in 1980, when the JOS went out of business. Since that time he had been unemployed. He found the occasional odd job but Mrs Smith, despite her age, was the chief breadwinner for her household.

Four of her seven children, ranging in age from twenty-one to twenty-seven years, lived with her, and she provided shelter and food for them because they were unskilled and usually unemployed. Three grandchildren also lived in her home and were provided for by her.

Of her children, only one son gave her any money on a regular basis, and that was only J$40 per month. (Forty dollars at that time was sufficient to buy one chicken and other supplies to provide a low-income family of five with three basic meals for one day.)

Mrs Smith had worked out of the home most of her life, as a domestic worker and for a number of years during the 1970s as an Impact Programme worker.[17] For the eight years prior to the survey she was self-employed in the "selling" trade. She explained this as follows. "A friend of mine goes to the United States and buys ready-made clothes, and then I walk around from house to house marketing the clothes and other items which are bought by the woman. It means I have to do a lot of walking up and down, but I can earn about J$2,000 per month."

She was unhappy about her relationship with her children, except with one of those who lived with her and the one who lived abroad. "These children have been a disappointment to me. They talk to me as if I'm their age; they show no respect and keep bad company," she said.

In terms of overall coping in Jamaica today, Mrs Smith said that her main problem was the high cost of food, for which she reckoned she spent in excess of J$600 per week. This cost represented only one bill, while her total income per week was J$1,000 on a "good week" and she still needed money to pay the electricity bill and provide lunch money and other necessities for her grandchildren.

Mrs Smith was an interesting woman, who showed her concern not only for her family but also for other women of the community in light of the escalating cost of living. She recognized that as a working woman she had difficulties coping with the economy, and feared for other women who had no income of their own.

For the past sixty years, domestic work has been, and continues to be, the most common form of employment for working-class women of Jamaica. It was also the main area of employment for the working-class women of this study. Women who worked as domestics did so for a number of reasons. The main reason was that it was the easiest employment to find. Also, for those who wanted to change, the opportunities did not always present themselves. The domestic helpers in this survey worked because their family needed their income, because their menfolk were unemployed and underemployed, and they were at times the sole provider for the family.

The case presented below shows a woman who worked as a domestic, and whose income, for years, had been vital to the survival of her family. She was prepared to take additional work on her weekly days off, to achieve her objectives. This was not an unusual situation and five other women of this study who worked as domestics sought additional employment on their days off.

Case No. 6

Mrs Williams, at age sixty-four years, had been working as a domestic all her adult life. Her first job was at age sixteen years. Like many other women, she had taken this type of job, as she said, "because it was the easiest job to get". She enjoyed her work and had actually worked for her current employer for thirty-five of those years.

At the time of the research she had been separated from her husband for twenty years. He had deserted the family after fourteen years of marriage. He had migrated to the United States, promising to send for the entire family and was never heard from. Mrs Williams was left to raise their five children, ranging in age from five to twelve years.

She said she was able to manage because of the emotional and material help she had received from her church. She was a devoted church-goer. She also stated that her employer had been very helpful to her and her children over the years. She was very pleased with her job as a domestic and said, "I really love this job. Without it I would not have been able to school my children."

It appears that her children did reasonably well in school. Three had migrated to the United States within the previous four years and she continued to support the two left behind in their bid to obtain further education. She was pleased with the progress these last two were making. She did not receive any financial assistance from the three who had migrated, because as she explained to me, "they have not settled as yet". This was to suggest to me that she expected that they would contribute financially to her household as soon as they had established themselves in the United States.

She earned J$300 (US$15 in 1991) per week and used that to support herself, her two youngest children and her eighty-two-year-old mother, who lived with them. Mrs Williams worked at an additional job on her day off in order to earn more income to support her children attending higher educational institutions.

A less expected reason why midlife and older women were out at work was that they wanted to make a contribution to the community. Such was the case for the two teachers whose stories are told below.

Case No. 7

Mrs Ramsay, at sixty-seven years, was a woman who could easily have passed for fifty-five. She was the mother of four sons ranging in age from thirty-two to forty years. She had been married for thirty-one years and widowed for ten years. Three of her sons were well-paid professionals: two worked abroad and one worked in a "high government office". The fourth son lived with her and was unemployed at the time. The unemployed son stated that he lived in the parental home with his mother because his brothers felt that their mother should not have to live alone. It also helped him financially to live at home, because rents were very high in the Kingston area and especially so in middle-class communities.

Mrs Ramsay had been a professional teacher for all her adult life and retired at age sixty years from a post as principal of a primary school in Kingston. Although retired she continued to lead a very active life. She taught twelve hours each week at a basic school not far from her home.[18] She did this not for the income, but because she felt she still had a contribution to make to the society. "I feel that it is important for women with skills and good health to help their community where there is need," she said. In addition to teaching, she was a member of the board of a number of educational and health institutions. She was a Parent Teacher Association counsellor, and a very active member of her church, sitting in executive positions on many of the church committees.

She acknowledged that the escalating cost of living was playing havoc with the lives of most of the people in Jamaica at the time, including middle-class persons and she too complained about the minuscule size of the government pension in relation to real costs. She noted, "the slightest bill, for example, a plumbing job, could run into thousands of dollars". As a consequence of the extremely high cost of food in the supermarkets, she stated, "I have cut down on many items. I now buy much less meat than before and I eat only very small pieces of it."

She stated that she was not allowing the inflation in the society to bother her. "My house was completely paid off, before my husband died, and I thank God for it, as I do not have a mortgage on it," she said. Unlike many of the other residents in the community, she had not extended her house by adding an apartment, but said she would do that in the near future, as it would be a source of income for her in her later years. She stated, "My sons would not see me want for anything. But I do not want to have to depend on them." (Her fourth son who was unemployed was funded by her oldest son.) She appeared to be very independent minded and courageous in spirit, but it did help that she had no major expenses to bear, no dependent children and good health.[19]

She stated that she knew the people in her community well, as she had lived in the area for more than twenty years and had served as advisor and confidante to many.

This case shows that although Mrs Ramsay was relatively secure financially, she continued to work out of the home because she wanted to make a contribution to the society. The next case shows another woman who wanted to make a contribution to the development of the young men of the society as well as earn a necessary income for herself and her family.

Case No. 8

Mrs Miller at age fifty-six years worked as a senior teacher in a boys' high school. She was the mother of four children who ranged in age from nineteen to thirty years. She had been married for thirty years and widowed for two. She had responsibility for two of her children who were still in higher educational institutions.

Her husband had also been a teacher, and she complained that they had never been able to live too comfortably on their combined salaries, and that they certainly had no savings. She was pleased though that they at least had a house that had been paid for, and she received her husband's pension. She stated that she needed to work because two children were still attending university. One daughter was employed and contributed to the household, but the oldest son lived abroad and was rarely heard from, and did not contribute financially.

She had this to say about her work: "The work is extremely demanding and the salary is low, but I feel that I get a chance to influence the lives of these boys not only in educational matters but because of the counselling which I do with them. I teach Advanced Level and also fifth form examination subjects. I have so many assignments to mark that these cannot be finished during school hours. I have to mark them at home, which is expensive, because my electricity bill becomes higher. The exercise is also potentially damaging to my vision."

Mrs Miller, although only fifty-six years old, expressed some serious reservations about growing older. She felt that growing older was a problem and that employers preferred to recruit from among the young. She might have been making specific comments about the teaching profession, as this reservation was not generally expressed.

Women of this age group often had no choice about whether or not they worked. Some also could not choose what type of work they did. Apart from the familial expectations that guided their work life, other constraints within the society also helped to determine what work would be available to them. Given these constraints and the fact that some worked out of the home when they would rather have stayed at home, one then has to be concerned about the satisfaction that they experienced in their jobs.

Job Satisfaction

Noteworthy responses with regard to sources of job satisfaction were: interaction with people, salary, being able to work from home and that the job was fulfilling. Hope Pastures women were more likely than August Town women to express satisfaction with their salaries, as well as general satisfaction with working. For example, Mrs Andrews (Respondent no. 115) at sixty-four years old was still in full-time employment as a senior secretary. She said, "I enjoy every moment of my work. I never take time off. I've been with the same company for twenty-eight years and the boss respects me and says he implements many of my ideas."

If we deal with satisfaction in employment, we should also seek to under-stand what women saw as the disadvantages of their work. Among the disad-vantages of their jobs that were mentioned were poor salaries and long working hours. Six per cent of the August Town sample and 19 per cent of the Hope Pastures sample complained about poor salaries. For 17 per cent of the August Town group who worked for an income, the major concern was the uncertainty of their income. This uncertainty would have been related to the informal nature of their employment or to their self-employment. Those women also expressed the desire to be more fully engaged in paid employment. Other problems mentioned were that there was no union (one respondent), no insurance (one respondent) and that people were reluctant to pay promptly for service given (three respondents). Here, reference was being made to jobs such as dressmaking and personal services, where clients would pay very late or not at all.

Although it was clear from the discussion that many women were unhappy with their salary, it was the middle-income women who were specific in their complaints about low salaries.[20] For them the inadequacy of their salary, accompanied by the rising cost of living, not only left them frustrated in their needs, which it did also for lower-income persons, but was seriously inhibiting them from maintaining the lifestyle that they had enjoyed in the past.

The issue of the employer/employee relationship was explored. I was concerned with the difference if any, that these women had observed in their employers' treatment of older persons in the workplace. It was my expectation, based on what was commonly heard in the society about older women's disadvantaged position in the workplace, that there would have been reports of discrimination. However, only a very small number of people, three from August Town and eleven from Hope Pastures, reported that they had observed any difference in the treatment of older workers.[21] Of these, nine persons reported that "older persons must work harder" and five persons reported that "younger persons received better salaries and conditions". The differences noted here for the two groups were not statistically significant. This suggests that generally these women did not feel particularly discriminated against in the workplace because of their age. The fact that such small numbers reported discrimination does not mean that it was infrequent, but suggests that midlife and older women had internalized and accepted the dominant discourse with regard to older women in the workforce and had anticipated and accepted whatever difficulties had arisen as they grew older in the workplace. One woman, however, complained bitterly about the treatment she had received at the hands of a banker when she had requested a loan. She eventually received the loan, but her son had to stand "surety" for her. She said, "I felt that I was being treated like a teenager; like a person who could not be trusted."

Non-Remunerated Work: Women's Low Perception of Their Own Work

Paid employment was, however, not the only type of work in which the women of this group were involved. Some women who did not work out of the home, as well as a few who had part-time employment outside the home, kept house for their grown daughters and sons, or kept their grandchildren of varying ages, as described in Case no. 1 in chapter 2. That respondent cared for her teenaged grandchildren; Respondent no. 2 minded one eleven-year-old, while

Respondent no. 12, like so many of these women, minded several children. Consequently, many households in both class groups were larger than anticipated because the women had incorporated additional family members, to cope better economically by pooling their resources. A similar phenomenon was noted by Duarte in the Dominican Republic.[22]

Besides being involved in paid employment, some of these women (eleven from August Town and twelve from Hope Pastures), before and after retirement took responsibility for their mothers, fathers and other relatives in their homes. Most did not think of this as work. This comes across very clearly in their responses in the case studies. For example Respondent no. 113 who, at age fifty-five years was employed in a senior nursing position, said, "Because I am the nurse in the family, I am expected to take care of our aged mother. It is not that I mind taking care of her, but my brothers and sisters just feel that the responsibility should be mine."

Another respondent was a well-known social worker and, apart from what she does for her family, she was very involved with many grassroots programmes that sought to improve the lives of people in low-income communities. This she did in her spare time, and in what should have been her family-time, but she stated, "It is something I have to do, it is not really work."

Respondent no. 2 had retired from a cleaning job but continued to work for an income by keeping boarders from the University of the West Indies and the College of Arts, Science and Technology. In addition to paid employment she had also taken care of her mother for ten years until she died in 1988 at the age of ninety-six years. Even at the time of the research, at sixty-eight, this lady took care of a ten-year-old boy she had "adopted" since his birth. She had been given him by his teenage mother. She saw her contribution to society as, to quote her, "The help I have given by 'raising' five children other than my own to adulthood."

The women in this survey were also in many ways involved in the "work" of their communities. Thirty-one August Town women and seventy-three Hope Pastures women stated that they were involved in specific activities in their communities, mainly as Sunday School teachers, family counsellors, members of church women's organizations, church leaders, visitors to the sick, members of citizens' organizations, members of neighbourhood watch organizations and members of political parties. A total of eight of the thirty August Town women

(25.8 per cent) and thirty-two of seventy-three Hope Pastures women (43.8 per cent) held executive positions in their various organizations.

Those women also helped younger women, who had to go out to work or had to leave their children at home at various points of the day, by minding those children who might otherwise have been left unattended or in the care of less responsible persons. By helping the younger women these women further established themselves as useful community citizens and so placed themselves in a better position to negotiate for favours, money and acts of reciprocity not yet thought of, but on which they would be able to "draw down" or count on in the future, because of the relationship that they had built up with other women in the community.

The Retired

A number of the women had retired but had gone back to work. The mean age at which these women of August Town and Hope Pastures had stopped working outside the home was 52.2 and sixty years, respectively. One such case was a seventy-year-old dress designer from the Hope Pastures community. She had retired formally but continued to work and also taught the art of dress designing to young women. Two other women from the August Town community shared their dressmaking skill with young women from their churches on a weekly basis.

At sixty-six years old, Respondent no. 164 had retired but had gone back to paid employment because four of her children depended on her in a number of different ways. Her husband was retired and very ill at home. She was the major income earner for herself, her husband, her four daughters and her eight grandchildren.[23]

This woman's life is a good illustration of the point that women, far from being "taken care of by family", as was sometimes suggested by the public officials I interviewed, were genuinely needed by their families, for their financial as well as their caregiving contributions.

Case No. 9

Mrs Gooden, of Hope Pastures, at the age of sixty-six years, led a very active life. She had been married for forty-one years and was the mother of eight children (six daughters and two sons) who ranged in age from twenty-seven to thirty-nine years.

She had worked almost all her adult years as an administrative secretary for the same organization. She had retired shortly before she was interviewed for this study but found that the cost of living at the time and the dependency of her children and grandchildren would not allow her to remain at home.

Of her eight children, four lived at home with her and in that regard she had this to say, "Two daughters never left home, so they are still living here. Two others had broken marriages and could not afford to pay rent elsewhere, so they and their four children (two each) returned here to live. Although I don't want them here, I still can't leave them to suffer." The two other daughters were secretaries and had been living in the United States, one for ten years and the other for twelve years.

Mrs Gooden presented herself as a very burdened and unhappy woman, who had worked all her life and who, on retirement, was forced to continue to work not because she wanted to but because her domestic situation required it. Her husband, a retired self-employed businessman, had been in very poor health since his retirement and earned no income other than his pension. He was also too ill to help around the house, and so she had all the responsibility in and around the home. She was employed as a companion to an elderly woman at nights, and by day she looked after her husband.

She found herself unable to speak kindly of her daughters or the grandchildren. She said, "The relationship with my daughters is not good at this time. They quarrel amongst themselves frequently and there is a lot of tension here, but they have nowhere else to go. They put a real strain on me. The grandchildren are disrespectful too and won't do what I tell them. My daughters are now grown-ups and yet I have to feed them and their children. I also pay all their bills for them without being reimbursed. They argue about who should do the chores, so I end up having to do most of the things myself. The grandchildren occasionally do some chores around the house." She added, "I have a better relationship with my sons than my daughters. With the girls there is too much worry and tension, but with the boys, I don't have to worry at all."

Mrs Gooden, although formally retired, had gone back to work as a "nurse" to an elderly woman. For this she earned J$1,500 per month. That sum was the most sizeable income that was coming into the house, and that income she said, "has to feed a family of ten". She said she was doing the best she could coping with the very difficult circumstances of her life. Food alone completely exhausted her salary, and money then had to be found to pay the utilities and house tax. She said, "I eat less and buy only what I can afford. I cut out extra things like plantains, potatoes and leave out ingredients which are not necessary in a meal. I can't eat as well as I used to. I have to budget very carefully now and buy only what is essential." At the time of the interviews she needed her car for her job and said, "I can hardly afford to keep my car on the road now."

She concluded that she was only able to cope because she made sacrifices for herself. She used her husband's small pension and her own smaller pension[24] to pay the additional bills, such as preparatory school fees for the four grandchildren and everything else that was required.[25] Her daughters, although low-paid secretaries, "are selfish with their salary", she says. She stated that they used all their income on themselves to attempt to keep up appearances and present fashionable images of themselves. They were, however, not financially independent and "would not be able to manage if they could not depend on me", she stated vehemently.

She concluded on a very sorry note, "Life has been pretty rough. Now that I am older, I want to rest, but I still have these 'grown-up' children and grandchildren to worry about."

She feared for the future somewhat, given the very high and escalating cost of living. She said she would like to be able to rent a part of her house to obtain some ready cash, but because the house was fully occupied with her daughters and grandchildren there was no space left that could be converted into a rentable unit within the home.

CONCLUSION

This chapter presented an overview of women and work and more specifically the work situation of some midlife and older women and the power relations influencing their work in and outside the home. The data showed that 128 of these 200 women were actually working for an income, but to meet with all of these women and to see them, was to be filled with a sense that their lives were still extremely active. There were some among the middle class whom I was able to meet and interview only in the evening because they continued to work long hours in their formal work schedules.

Although women nowadays have a wider range of occupations to choose from, there was a gendered division of labour that restricted them to a smaller range of occupations than their menfolk. Within this survey the working-class women especially were restricted by this division. This directs us to the importance of class within the society. The difference between the range of occupations for middle-class women and middle-class men was not nearly so stark.

Most of these women who were in paid employment had no choice but to work. Even middle-class women were out at work, not merely for the continuity of their careers, though this would have been the case for some, but for the majority it was because their salaries were required for attempting to maintain the integrity of their individual domestic economy. Some were also employed because they did not want to accept the view that non-employment is normal at their age.

The women in this research did what they saw as necessary for the maintenance of the economic and social stability of their family and household; despite all they did, those around them did not take full cognisance of their activities. It was certainly not that these women sought to be recognized or given any special accord or reverence for their work. In talking to them it was clear that this was not their desire. They did what they had to do unselfishly and unstintingly because to them this was all part of their coping role whether or not it was recognized. Self-negation was what these women practised without perhaps even being aware of it. It was important for them to keep the entire family nurtured and assisted, even at great cost to themselves in terms of time and money. This is how they were constituted in the dominant societal discourses. Discourses are powerful and they lived their lives as they were expected to do.

Women here, as in other areas of their lives, did not offer much resistance to the dominant societal discourses that do not acknowledge the extent of their contribution. Theirs was not a "trumpet-blowing" group. One came to the realization of exactly what was their contribution to family and community only if one worked directly with them or asked specific questions of them.

Those women took on the apparently never-ending obligations and duties that go with mothering in Jamaica. They accepted the hegemonic ideologies in relation to their multiple roles in the society. They did not always welcome these obligations, but saw no escape from the deteriorating economic situation, which left their spouses and children sometimes unemployed, and their pensions of less and less value. All of this, coupled with their lack of a language in which their desire to be free of these burdens could legitimately be expressed, left them willing but reluctant: ambivalent victims of a lifetime of labour. Their lack of a language of resistance meant they could only blame their children if they were not happy: daughters who burdened their homes and sons who did not contribute enough financially. Yet their problems were really set much deeper within the constraints placed by the structures of the wider society, such as an unemployment rate of 20 per cent in Jamaica in 1991.

An understanding of the ways in which discourses, or perhaps the lack of them, constrain women's lives is useful in making sense of the data presented in this chapter. So many women, not a majority, but too many, expressed dissatisfaction with their never-ending low status. Some middle-class women found their working lives rewarding, but most from both groups found that despite their best efforts they still experienced life as short-changing them. They did the best they could but their work was not taken seriously nor seen as important by those around them.

CHAPTER 4
WOMEN, HEALTH
AND THE REPRESSED DISCOURSE

Mrs Brown was always busy. She worked full-time as an administrative officer in a non-governmental organization. She was involved in a number of community organizations and was active as an executive committee member in some of these organizations. She was the main financial contributor to her home and a companion to her retired husband, who was recovering from surgery for colon cancer. She travelled abroad several times each year to attend conferences and to visit her two daughters who live in the United States. At age sixty-four, Mrs Brown is an active and highly respected member of her community and the Jamaican society. Mrs Brown is a stark reminder to us that growing older does not equate with illness. Many older persons do have health problems, but even larger numbers do not.
— *Respondent no. 139*

INTRODUCTION

This chapter analyses the health status of Jamaican women at midlife and older, and the power relations that affected their lives as they sought to ensure health care for themselves. A brief overview of the organization of the Jamaican health service as it existed in 1990–91, and its operation, will help us to better appreciate how women managed their health, given the restructuring of the health services mentioned in chapter 1. This chapter argues that, despite the women's need to remain in good health in order to fulfil their various roles, the health-care system did not provide adequately for them. The chapter also argues that because of the power relations within the family and the wider society, women quite often did not see themselves as ill when they were; that their relatives also did not perceive them as ill, and did not expect them to be ill, especially if they were less than sixty years old. The discourses that surrounded these women's lives, especially those in the younger age group, were that they were well and able. Additionally, the power relations at the micro and macro levels created a situation in which these women provided some amount of health care for family and community members without much support from family and the state.

The health of women of this age group is really very important because they make a significant contribution to the society, as has been demonstrated in previous chapters. If their health is not maintained or if they have no resources to deal with health problems when these arise, they will not be able to perform adequately the various roles that they have in the society. These women worked outside the home as well as in the home. As such, their families and extended families depended on them, because their incomes were still needed, they were responsible for the organization of their homes on a daily basis, and in some cases because they were responsible for the care of young children in their homes, as well as the care of older people. It would seem obvious that if they were so involved in the productive and reproductive activities of the family, they should be in a state of health that would enable them to perform their roles to their own satisfaction and without damaging their health status.

Until recent times women, and indeed men, did not live to the advanced ages that they do today. Nowadays, the life expectancy for women and men has increased and consequently also the need to pay attention to their health and other needs, such as the provisions for work, and for their welfare in the society. The United Nations, in full recognition of the so-called greying of the world's population, has sought to monitor the health of such persons. With this in mind, this research also looked briefly at the situation of the health of midlife and older women in the international context, in order to then place the health situation of Jamaican women in a wider context.

Studies of midlife and older women in industrialized countries indicate that health and well-being are in many ways similar for older persons in these various nations. These studies show that the majority of older persons are in good health with no significant mental or physical decline. Only about 8 per cent of older people are seriously impaired or dependent on extensive health care. The most pressing and treatable problems of older people throughout the world are related to heart function, hearing, teeth, diabetes, visual impairment and osteoporosis (UN 1992).[1] Studies of older women in developing countries show a wider variation in the status of women's health.

MORBIDITY AND MORTALITY IN THE CARIBBEAN

If one considers health, one must also consider the causes of morbidity and consequently mortality. The reasons for mortality among midlife and older women, as reported by Sennott-Miller (1989, 82), are outlined below. She showed the five major causes of death for midlife and older women in Latin America in the 1980s as malignant neoplasms, followed by heart disease, cerebrovascular disease, diabetes, and accidents. In women beyond that age, heart disease, followed by cerebrovascular disease, are the first and second main causes of deaths. Similar patterns were noted for the Caribbean, with the difference being that chronic liver disease "appears to be a much greater problem in the Caribbean among the 45- to 64-year-old women than in Latin America" (Sennot-Miller 1989, 85).[2] Where gender differences were concerned, despite the high ranking of cardiovascular and cerebrovascular diseases in women's mortality, death rates are still higher among men, particularly in the urban communities (PAHO 1985, 114). Sennott-Miller (1989, 85) noted that beginning at about age thirty-five and continuing through midlife and beyond, malignancies rank first as causes of death. Among these, two types of cancers, breast and uterine cervix, are by far the greatest killers. In the main developing countries of Latin America and the Caribbean, breast cancer was more common (Senott-Miller 1989; Singh 2002). The situation with regard to mortality for this age group remains much the same in the Caribbean (Eldemire 2002) with some small change due to the increase in mortality from HIV/AIDS-related complications for those closer to age fifty years (Rawlins 2002b).

It is important to make reference to diabetes and hypertension, as the available data show that they are among the most frequently occurring potentially life-threatening conditions that affect Caribbean populations. In Jamaica, it was estimated that there were 120,000 diabetics in the population in 1990–91 (Statistical Institute of Jamaica 1990b), and diabetes is cited as increasing throughout Latin America and the Caribbean. Within the Caribbean it is particularly severe and "is believed to affect between 8 per cent to 10 per cent of the adult population, and account for 15 per cent to 20 per cent of the hospital bed occupancy" (PAHO 1985). Because of its association with overweight, Caribbean women, who tend to be more overweight than Caribbean men, are even more prone to diabetes and hypertension (Burke 1983).[3]

Many studies have been done in the Caribbean to attempt to determine the causes of the incidence of these diseases, for example, those of Waldron, Nowotarski and Friemer (1982), Dressler (1992), Whitbourne (1999) and Morrison et al. (2001). The Dressler study was done in Gordon Town, a community on the outskirts of Kingston, Jamaica. There Dressler found significant differences by class and gender in the probability of high blood pressure. He concluded that social class differences in blood pressure for males are mediated by perceptions of social support, while social class differences in blood pressure for females was mediated by perceptions of economic stress. This means that men were less likely to be hypertensive if they had a sense of having support from friends, colleagues and the church, while women were less likely to be hypertensive if they had a sense that they were able to manage their domestic economy without feeling that they were under excessive stress.

Although the evidence on the causation of high blood pressure is inconclusive, the importance of stress cannot be ruled out of its aetiology. If this is a factor, then the years of cumulative stress in the lives of many Jamaican and Caribbean women as they have attempted to cope with the difficult social and economic circumstances, which have been especially severe for at least the last two decades, would make them ideal candidates for development of the disease.

Where diabetes is concerned, the high-fat and high-carbohydrate diet for many low-income families can probably be implicated. This type of diet is often linked to women's desire to provide more of the "meat", and thus the protein, for the man of the house, leaving mainly the carbohydrate for themselves, which they use as fillers, and which provides them with inadequate nutrition.[4] They see the men as more important, at least at the table and so provide them with more of the protein foods.

Another health problem that has been identified for some women of this age group is that of anaemia. This form of anaemia arises from an inadequate diet over time, compounded by having large numbers of children. This anaemia leads to a decrease in quantity and quality of circulating red cells. Sennott-Miller (1989, 93) from her work in the region concluded that "nutritional anaemia affects large numbers of adult women in the Latin American region, and that its long-term effects can be devastating in terms of productivity and general health". Alleyne (2000) makes a similar point about Caribbean women's anaemic status.[5]

THE JAMAICAN HEALTH-CARE SYSTEM

Health care is an expensive commodity, whether it is provided privately or by the government, but more so if provided privately. For this reason the majority of Jamaicans receive most of their health care from the sector that is financed through government funds. The government, through the Ministry of Health, in 1990–91 managed twenty-four public hospitals and over 350 health clinics. Each of the fourteen parishes into which the country is divided had at least one public hospital and several health centres, which implies that, in theory, service is always a reasonable distance from the population. Jamaica up to the mid-1970s had managed to provide adequate health care for its population. In this regard Levitt (1991, 49) states: "among countries of comparable income Jamaica has long enjoyed an enviable record in the provision of public health . . . services".

Health care in Jamaica during 1990–91 was not without its difficulties. Very heavy demands were being placed on both public and private sectors, and both sectors at times were having difficulties coping, because of the attrition of health professionals and because of shortage of other resources. Levitt (1991, 51) comments on this mass exodus of medical personnel into private practice locally and abroad as follows:

> In 1971, there was one physician in the public sector for every 2,678 persons; in 1980 the situation had deteriorated to one physician for every 3,035 persons; and by 1988 the physician to population ratio was 5,240. The ratio of nursing personnel to population in 1975 was one nurse for every 646 persons; and by 1985 the nurse to population ratio was 1,172.

There can be no doubt that the deterioration in the staffing situation of the health service would have adversely affected the service provided. We reflect on the fact that it is often said that the health status of a population reflects the general level of welfare in a country. It is therefore important to note the following comment, which was made about the Jamaican population in 1990: "Health status of the population is showing signs of increasing stress. Cardio-vascular diseases, diabetes, psychiatric diseases, respiratory tract infections all appear to be on the increase, but the ability of the Ministry of Health to respond though has been reduced" (Planning Institute of Jamaica 1990, section 20.1).

The available data suggested that annually, for at least the decade prior to the research for this study, the sum allocated to the health ministry from the government's budget was inadequate. It is commonly said in Jamaica that the percentage of the overall budget that is allocated to health each year should have been more.[6] Several studies, including those by Stevens (1983) and Cumper, Walker and McCormack (1985) found that the Ministry of Health was under-financed and concluded that health care would be adversely affected. Under-financing has been identified as one of the major problems confronting the Jamaican health sector. The World Health Organization (WHO) recommends that a minimum of 5 per cent of the gross domestic product (GDP) be spent on health services in order to provide the respective populations with the basic health coverage, but for Jamaica, in the years immediately prior to this research, this target has not been realized and Levitt (1991, 51) notes, "Capital expenditure for health declined from 10.4 per cent of total public health expenditure in 1981/82 to an all time low of 3.7 per cent in 1985/86."[7]

There was no doubt, however, that the adverse changes that had taken place in the government health sector since the mid-1970s and the additional changes in the 1980s in relation to structural adjustment (see chapter 1) had negative effects on the population. Those most affected were the poor, as they were the ones who had no alternative but to use that sector of the health service. In reference to this fact Levitt (1991, 52) writes:

> It is the poor who have to suffer the deterioration of public health-care facilities. The *Survey of Living Conditions* shows that 55 per cent of the population go to private doctors' offices where they pay an average of $54 per visit, while 42 per cent use the deteriorating and understaffed public facilities (out-patient clinics and public health centres) where the cost per visit is only $4.

Midlife and Older Women

SPECIAL PROVISIONS

Given the limitations of the health services, which were widely publicized in 1990–91 and which all users had come to know, this researcher was concerned to know what midlife and older women would expect of the service and whether or not they were seen and treated as a special group in the way that the maternal and child health clients are seen as a special group. Having spoken to various health professionals in Jamaica it was clear that women of this age group were not perceived as a special group in need of particular care within the health-care system.[8] In the area of menopause, the discourse seemed limited. Evident in the discourse was a silencing, a "black-out", on menopause. It would seem that older women were not seen as key factors to the economy and society and there was no perceived need to be overly concerned with menopause, which did not affect supposedly more pivotal workers, such as men and younger women.

The special programmes within the public health-care service in 1990–91 were those that tended to cater to younger groups, such as maternal and child health, family planning and schoolchildren. There were programmes within limited areas that sought to assess the hypertensive status of older people, but those were not intensive programmes; they did not cater to the specific needs of women, and midlife and older women could very easily have fallen outside of the screening process.

Midlife and older women were not treated as a special group because there was no recognition that they constituted a group requiring attention and the resources available to the Ministry of Health were not sufficient to enable them to be treated as such. They were also not perceived as a powerful lobby by the politicians in the way that members of the workforce might have been perceived. However, women of this age group do form a special group, at least as far as some of them were concerned, and especially with regard to their health. One woman, for example, asked, "In what age-group would you find so many hypertensives, diabetics, overweight persons and people with arthritis?" Another respondent added, "We are also the group which is going through the change." Although most did not see the "change" as a major problem, some felt it would have been good to have been able to talk to a health professional about it.

HEALTH AND THE WOMEN IN THE SAMPLE

What was clear from the data gathered was that despite these women's need to keep in good health, the circumstances of their lives, their family and the state did not provide adequately for them, nor did these circumstances encourage them to take time out to ensure that their health was properly maintained.

It was going to be very difficult for these women to remain in good health, if the health authorities had decided that only limited service should be available to this age group, that such women were not particularly productive perhaps, and that the available resources were needed elsewhere, and so were not made available to provide adequate care for older women. These women had ideas about the status of their own health, and their health-care needs. Some of them for example spoke of their "nerves". (I would be surprised to find any mention of these "nerves" in any medical text.) These needs and what they knew for sure about their health in some cases had no voice, had not been expressed, and were in effect repressed discourses; consequently their needs went unmet at times.

The data showed that close relatives made demands on the time of these women based on the assumption that these women were in sufficiently good health to be able to meet the daily requests of their relatives without having to take time out to see to their own health needs. The women also, perhaps because of these relations and because they wanted to be seen as able and coping well, tended not to see themselves as unwell even when they were, or they understated their illness conditions. The case study reported on in this chapter in which the diabetic and hypertensive woman recovering from a mastectomy was out and about at work is a case in point. See also the case of Mrs Steadman below.

The following quotation from a respondent, which was a typical response, indicated women's attitudes towards their health in a situation in which the daily relations with their relatives forced them to cope. "I'm as strong as an ox. There is nothing wrong with me except the 'pressure'," said one respondent. She was referring to the fairly serious and sometimes life-threatening condition of hypertension. Yet she did not really see herself as ill nor did she complain because, as Graham (1982, 114) has said, to complain is not to cope. This particular woman was intent on coping. She had her job to do and her family to organize. To complain unduly about her headache and other related hypertensive symptoms would be to draw attention to herself, to have others see her as sick, and perhaps to risk her job as a domestic servant, which she needed and on which her family depended for an important contribution to the family's budget. In effect, she did not want to create for herself a situation that was not in keeping with the dominant discourse on women of her age.

Most of the women lived out their lives in a situation in which no one expected them to be ill or in need of health care.[9] The following are excerpts from taped conversations with two of the women. One Hope Pastures respondent (Case no. 26) had experienced years of stress in relation to her family circumstances and was recovering from a nervous breakdown when she was first interviewed for the survey. She said: "I have not been very well. I'm still under medication from my doctor. I have been under a great deal of stress since I went back out to work. My husband lost his job and the job I have is entirely different from the jobs I did in the past. I feel very insecure in it, but I am now the breadwinner, so I can't afford to stay at home. Life is very stressful right now."

Here was a middle-class woman who, at fifty-six years of age, had to return to the workforce because of changed economic circumstances within her household. There were bills to be paid, a car to maintain and children in college. Her health was already at risk and was being further endangered because of the conditions under which she had to work and because of the numerous unresolved difficulties within her family.

Another respondent (Case no. 9) who was interviewed at her workplace, said, "I'm at work today although I do not feel very well because of the problems with my fibroids. I'm under treatment from the gynaecologist at the University Hospital, for the problem and anaemia. The heavy bleeding, for up to as many as twelve days, has 'checked' a little but I still have this burning pain in my side. But apart from these things I'm in good health."

Here was a woman with a disruptive gynaecological problem, who did not think it was necessary to take time out from work, or who was unable to take time out of work, and so pressed on despite her condition. She also stated that she had not been encouraged by any of her family to take time out from work.

The contention that no one expects such women to be ill is supported by Popay (1992), who concluded that women did not perceive themselves as having freedom to be ill; this view appeared to be shared by their husbands. Husbands, in Popay's research, by and large, did not expect the wives to take time out from the various tasks they had to perform, to be ill.

In the research for this study, it was interesting to note how very few of these women admitted that they were ill. In fact, maybe because of their inner determination, or because they did take care of themselves in ways that we do not quite understand, many of them were in very good health. But we must note a somewhat troubling factor in that even those who were not well and who in fact reported incidences of ill health, such as diabetes or hypertension, also reported themselves to be in good health. We note for example the respondent who reported herself to be "as strong as an ox". Careful examination of the health information she provided revealed that she was seriously hypertensive. She was aware of the seriousness of the condition, in that she stated that she attended the hypertensive clinic on a three-monthly basis. She took her medicines as was prescribed – but did not think of herself as a sick person, and did not take to her bed, or seek to be treated by relatives and neighbours as sick.

The research led me to conclude that the discourse on the health of women of this age group allows for "sick" women and "well" women but not for women who were not in perfect health, but were still able to function. As a result of this lack of fit between the discourse and the women's experienced reality, women who were not in perfect health behaved as if they were. In so doing they were collaborating with the dominant discourse, instead of presenting counter-discourses which would show that many women of this age group, although not in perfect health, do function as "near healthy" persons because of the relationships in which they find themselves and the realities of their life situation.

The case study below highlights further what women had to say of their own health and how they had accepted the health care that was available to them. This was a typical situation. The case also indicates that these women's health was of no particular concern to anyone apart from themselves and they behaved as if they knew they could not afford to be ill.

Case No. 10

Mrs Steadman was fifty-two years old and the mother of five children. She had lived at a number of different addresses in August Town over the past nineteen years but had lived at her current address for the past ten years. Prior to living in August Town she had lived in West Kingston. Her house was one of four in a tenement yard. The house was situated immediately behind a small shop, which was the closest building to the road. The shop was owned and operated by one of the other tenants in the yard.

Mrs Steadman and her husband owned their house, but not the land, which was leased from the landlord. The house was wooden and had five small bedrooms, a dining room, a living room and a verandah. Besides her husband and herself all the five children lived at home. One daughter was married and her husband and two children also resided there.

Mrs Steadman's story was particularly remarkable in that her husband had separated himself from her and the children for ten of the twenty years of their marriage, and had only returned to the family home in the year prior to the interview. At the time he had left, the children ranged in age from six to eighteen years. She had this to say of him, "He returned not because we wanted him to, but now that he is older he feels he needs us. The truth is that he needs us much more than we need him. He is afraid that when he grows older and becomes ill he will have no one to look after him and that the children will remember what he did and refuse to help him. He works as a maintenance man but his contribution to the family is so meagre, J$70 per week. I really don't know why he bothers as there is nothing much that you can do with J$70."

When asked about her health Mrs Steadman replied that she was in reasonably good health, and was happy about it as she would not know how to manage with the high cost of prescription medication. She said she suffered from hypertension, which at the time was under control, and she also stated she had been treated a number of times for urinary tract infections. She also added, "I'm glad that I do not have 'anything' that will cause me to be admitted to the hospital, as I can't afford to go to a private hospital, and from what I have seen and heard of the Public Hospital, I would not want to go there.[10] I'm so glad that I do not have to take time off from work for sickness. The only time I do not go to work is when I need to take a morning off to attend the hypertension clinic and that is rare because I work only four days each week and I usually go to the clinic on the day that I do not work." Mrs Steadman, at the time, worked as a domestic helper; the only type of employment she had held all her adult life. She said she enjoyed her job as her employers were "decent Christian people". She earned J$500 per month and supplemented her full-time employment with the proceeds from selling pastries, which she made at her home and sold on her days off and on weekends.

An important point to note about Mrs Steadman's situation was that she considered herself to be in good health despite her hypertension and urinary tract infections. She was concerned not to be ill, not only because she needed to be out at work but because she was aware of the inadequacies of the health service, and the fact that she would receive no benefits if she became ill and had to stay at home.

That Mrs Steadman's husband returned to the marital home is in keeping with what would have been expected of a married older woman.[11] Older women are expected to take care of and provide for any family member who needs such care, as long as they are physically able. Her husband was therefore returning to the household, so that he would be close to the perennial family caregiver in the event of his ill health.

The women in this survey were quite willing to talk about the health of women of their age group, in general, and their own health specifically. The data revealed that the majority of the women of both groups, that is, 79 per cent of the August Town women and 91 per cent of the Hope Pastures women described their health as good or fairly good. For both groups, only a small percentage (8 per cent for August Town and 6 per cent for Hope Pastures) described their health as bad. For both groups, the women who described their health as bad were those sixty to seventy-four years old.

The women were asked a question that sought information about their past health. This was important because past health invariably impacts on one's present health status. In relation to their personal involvement in any major illness or surgery, 26 per cent of the August Town sample and 47 per cent of the Hope Pastures sample reported that they had had serious illnesses and surgery in the past. We note that many more of the Hope Pastures women had surgery and serious illnesses. It is highly unlikely that these women would have been the victims of poorer health leading to illness and requiring surgery, but the more likely the explanation would be that more middle-income women were treated for their problems, which were diagnosed as serious, and that more had surgical intervention. For example the data reveal that 22 per cent of the Hope Pastures women had had hysterectomies compared with 6 per cent of the August Town women, and that 10 per cent of the Hope Pastures women compared to 6 per cent of the August Town women had had surgery for a number of unspecified conditions. So we see from the data the higher incidence of surgical intervention among the middle-class sample.[12] Among those who mentioned the type of surgery they had, these included three mastectomies, four gall bladder operations and three stomach ulcers. These surgical operations were spread fairly evenly across the two groups.

Midlife and Older Women

For the purposes of the research, it was important to try to separate out the reports of illness mentioned by these women and to determine which ones had occurred after they arrived at the point in their life cycle that is the focus of this study, because we were concerned to know

TABLE 2

Serious Illness or Surgery Experienced by Community Group

	August Town	Hope Pastures	Total
	No.	No.	No.
Before age 50 years	13	20	33
Since age 50 years	13	27	40
No serious illness/surgery	54	53	107
Not stated	20	–	20
Total	100	100	200

if any of their ill health had happened in their younger years, which then would have led family and community to see them as dependent and unable to contribute meaningfully to the family. The various conditions that the groups reported as affecting them since the age of fifty years included gynaecological problems, hypertension, cardiac problems, stomach and gall bladder, arthritis and problems with vision. Table 3 shows that these women suffered health conditions that should have been properly represented in the dominant discourses on ill health, chief among them hypertension, diabetes and arthritis.

Arthritis is a potentially crippling disease, which requires that the affected person have a regular source of painkillers. Given the high cost of medication, it means that those who did not have access to such drugs at no cost would have to endure the pain associated with their condition. The data showed that a total of 18 per cent and 15 per cent of the August Town and Hope Pastures samples, respectively, suffered from arthritis.

As a group, those suffering from hypertension were the most striking, with fifty-four persons reporting themselves as hypertensive. Of the thirty-nine August Town women who were

TABLE 3

Current Health Status by Community Group

	August Town	Hope Pastures	Total
	No.	No.	No.
No problem	24	23	47
Fibroids	2	3	5
Arthritis	18	15	33
Diabetes	10	11	21
Hypertension	39	15	54
Eye disease	4	4	8
Headache/dizziness	3	1	4
Cardiac problems	1	0	1
Other	8	18	26
Not stated	16	10	26

hypertensive, fifteen were also diabetic, while two of the fifteen Hope Pastures women were also diabetic. This naturally had serious implications for the health of these women, as the two conditions have adverse side effects and, together, constitute special risks to the individual's long-term health. Significantly, sixteen of the fifty-four hypertensive women (29.6 per cent) responded to their health status as if it were not a particularly important or potentially serious condition. They said, for example: "Oh! My health is good, I only have the 'pressure'", or, "I'm fine apart from a little pressure." These women's apparent lack of acknowledgement of the seriousness of their condition was perhaps related to the frequency of its occurrence in their community and in the population in general.

However, some of the women genuinely had no health problems, as we see from Table 4. Even then, whether or not they were ill, they could have ensured by their resistance through the presentation of active counter-discourses about their health that at least preventive health care for all of them could be assured.

Most of those who reported no health problems were in the age range fifty to fifty-nine years (Table 4).[13] Generally, this younger group reported fewer current health problems. These women were in reasonably good health because they were aware of the need to visit their doctor at least once annually; 69 per cent of the August Town women and 70 per cent of the Hope Pastures women stated that they visited their doctors at least that frequently. Naturally those who were hypertensive and diabetic and those who reported serious health conditions paid more regular visits to their doctors or health centres. Twenty-two of the women, ten from August Town and twelve from Hope Pastures, stated that they needed to visit their doctors at least every three months.

TABLE 4
Health Condition by Age

Illness	Age (years)		Total
	50–59	60–74	No.
No problem	47	–	47
Hypertension	8	46	54
Diabetes	2	19	21
Arthritis	–	33	33
Eye disease	–	–	8
TOTAL	57	99	156

When asked directly whether or not older women need to check on their health regularly, 81 per cent of the August Town women and 93 per cent of the Hope Pastures women replied in the affirmative. Only 3 per cent and 4 per cent of the women of the two groups stated that older women only needed to check on their health if they felt unwell. Thus, there was a good understanding of preventive medicine, and these women gave some indication of the special areas into which physical checks should be made, such as gynaecological tests and regular pap smears, breast and blood pressure examinations, urine and vision testing. The data revealed that these women were not only stating what they believed was the ideal about women's need to check on their health, but had themselves attended for these health checks. The majority of these women, 74 per cent of the August Town and 84 per cent of the Hope Pastures sample, had visited their doctors or health centres for physical examinations within the past twelve months.

It was interesting to note that the lower-income group appeared to make as good use of the health service as the middle-income group. The latter group had insurance or paid privately for their health care, while the former tapped into the available governmental services. I need to note though that the lower-income women of the study in relation to their health would not have been typical of all women of similar age in Jamaica, as these women had the special benefits of living in a community that was only a short distance away from a special health centre.

One of the greatest differences noted between the two groups relating to their health and their approach to treatment was how the women dealt with the issue of uterine fibroids, which is fairly common in the Jamaican population in women over forty years old. Within the lower-income group, the women dealt with the problems of menorrhagia (excessive menstrual loss) by staying at home and coping with the inconvenience themselves over many years. The middle-class women resolved the problem first through hormone treatment and then through surgical intervention. Consequently, in the middle-class community there were many more women who had had hysterectomies than among the women in the lower-income community. This was one particular situation in which the response to illness was different for the women of the two income groups.[14]

The issue of menopause is important because of the particular age group of this study, and this is addressed in some detail in the case studies. In the Caribbean, as elsewhere, there are myths about the subject, not the least of which is that women lose their interest in sex and sexual matters after the onset of menopause. For many of these women, however, menopause was merely another readily manageable life event, such as menarche, or the experience of first childbirth. Most of the women who spoke about it had taken menopause in their stride. These findings are similar to those of Wilson (1992) for Trinidad. There were a few, mainly those with fewer years of education, who seemed to be somewhat confused about the power and the potentially harmful effects of menopause. For example one said, "I'm told it could kill you." The majority of those who referred to it had more sober views as to its potential, and some remarked that more could be done by the Ministry of Health and their local clinics to educate women more about it, so that they would be better able to anticipate its effects on their health and their life in general. But it was not only less educated women who had been surprised by some events during this period of the change. One woman, a health worker, had had a total hysterectomy after several years of menorrhagia. She stated, "I really don't feel like myself anymore since I had the hysterectomy. I was never anti-hysterectomy, but no one told me that a total hysterectomy could make me feel so 'woozy', so unlike myself, so shaky." She felt that the surgeon should have explained to her more carefully about the difference having a total hysterectomy would make to her life, at least in the early period after the operation, and that it would take more than the usual six weeks for her to feel better.[15] Her ovaries had been removed, and she said, "I felt that my hormones had gone crazy, making me feel very bad indeed."

It was obvious to this researcher that women in the study were concerned about their own health, but were there other persons or agencies concerned about the maintenance of their health? I sought to find out from them what, if anything, was being done for them to promote health for their age group. There were two specific questions. The first was: "Is there anything that you know of that the Ministry of Health or your local clinic does specifically for women of your age group?" The second question was: "Is there anything that you think that the Ministry of Health or your local clinic should be doing specially for women of your age group?" For most of the women from both groups the responses to the first question were extremely vague. In fact, most stated that nothing was being done. The August Town women, however, especially those who attended the local Social and Preventive Medicine Clinic, stated that a number of things were being done for them, such as the holding of weekly hypertensive and diabetic clinics. However, in relation to the second question, the answers were more revealing.

Fifty-one per cent of the August Town sample, and 71 per cent of the Hope Pastures sample mentioned various things that the Ministry of Health or their local clinic could do specifically for women of fifty to seventy-four years. The data showed that the differences in the response from the two groups were statistically significant. The suggestions included that special clinics should be held for this age group, that there should be more education about the menopause, and that clinics should be organized to minimize the waiting time that currently exists at the health centres and that there should be a specially reduced price for the medicines required by the women of this age group.

The women also expressed the belief that if more was done by the Ministry of Health and local clinics for women of this age group it would encourage the women to take better care of their health, that preventive care would save more money for the government and the country in the long run, and that women would then have a better understanding of the changes that take place in their bodies in relation to menopause, and with this better understanding would be healthier and happier women. More knowledge would also empower them in coping with life in this phase of their life cycle in which many aspects of their lives were different. It would be good for them to be confident about this aspect of their lives.

With regard to what the government could do for them, the women said, for example:

> "The government could provide more education for women about their health and also set up counselling clinics for older people."

> "They could encourage women to go regularly for their tests."

> "They could have better medical facilities, as it puts a great strain on older people when they have to deal with poor health facilities."

> "The government takes on teenage pregnancy and some problems of the elderly, but no one cares about the middle group, although we have a lot of emotional problems."

This last comment was made by a fifty-six-year-old woman. Another woman had this to say, "More doctors should be encouraged into the field of geriatrics. There is so much to understand, and very few medical people really understand older people."

However, although these women made these comments, specifically because they were asked, it would seem that their views formed part of a repressed discourse that the health authorities did not know about. These views were in essence a discourse that the Ministry of Health and the medical profession "could not hear", as it differed from the official view that was held: that women of this age group have no special health needs that had to be addressed, over and above the health needs of other groups.

FAMILY, HEALTH AND THE REPRESSED DISCOURSE

The case presented below shows a woman whose access to power within her family and community was minimal, resulting in a situation in which, despite her best efforts over the years, she remained in ill health and unhappy.

Case No. 11

Mrs Wright (Respondent no. 31) was a widowed woman aged sixty years. She had been married for thirty-seven years and had been a widow for five years. She was a most unhappy-looking woman, who presented herself as a woman with all the cares of the world on her. She was very thin and appeared somewhat malnourished.

She was the mother of four children, two sons and two daughters, ranging in age from twenty-five to forty years. She lived in her own house, which had been the family house for the past thirty years. She owned the house, but the land had been leased from the government. She stated that she shared the house with her twenty-five-year-old daughter and a grandchild, and her son who was twenty-nine years old, in order to keep the cost down. She added though that her daughter contributed nothing to the house, and her son contributed only very little each month, because he complained that he could give no more from the very small salary he earned as a messenger. Although they did not make a meaningful financial contribution, they bought the food that was eaten in the house, and in exchange Mrs Wright helped to mind the grandchild when her daughter was not at home.

She, like Mrs Steadman (Case no. 10), had also worked as a domestic servant all her life. Her jobs had not given her any pleasure, and she had done them reluctantly. She, like so many women of her age and class, had had primary education only, but she felt she had deserved more than domestic work but had never been able to find anything "better" to do. She presented a picture of a woman who had been unhappy all her life and who had felt that she had been cheated by life. She had been unemployed for the past ten years because of ill health.

She was hypertensive and suffered from arthritis and it was the hypertension that had finally caused her to give up paid employment. She had not been happily married and she said, "I had so many worries all of my life until I began to suffer with my 'nerves'. I used to worry about my children. I worried about my husband. I worried about my health. I just worried and worried all the time. I still worry about the children and myself. I worry about the house, which is in need of repairs and we have no money to do it. I worry about the lack of money and that my children do not give me any. I also worry about the cost of living and I also worry about the society. It is not a kind one to old people. As soon as you get old no one wants to know you."

Here was a woman who appeared more downtrodden than any other woman I had met during the course of the research. She had worked hard for her children, but concluded society, and supposedly family, had not been kind to her as an older person; that society was not kind to older persons generally. Even her attempts to continue to share her life and home with her children were not working to her advantage. Clearly, if she had ever seen her children as investments for the future she had been disappointed. She was completely vulnerable and apparently defeated by the circumstances of her life. Whatever power Mrs Wright could exercise, those around her had more, and she was able to use very little of her power to her advantage. Although she lived in a house that she owned outright, the fact that she had been unemployed for years and had no savings placed her in an unfortunate relationship with her children, on whom she depended for financial assistance. But her children were caught up in their own difficult economic situation, and consequently could not provide her with the type of support that would have made her life more comfortable. Thus, her problems were created largely by factors such as her unemployment, lack of savings and the underemployment of her children.

Mrs Wright's relationship with the wider community provided her with no solace. Although she was a widow, she did not receive a widow's benefit from the state. She also did not receive NIS benefits, although she had worked as a domestic helper for years. Her employer had clearly not made the necessary arrangements to ensure that she would receive her benefits. Hers was not a unique situation and many women had been afraid to approach their middle-class employers in this regard because they were afraid to lose their badly needed employment. They preferred not to have their NIS cards stamped than to lose out on employment.[16]

It was as if the circumstances of their lives at the time dictated that they show less concern for long-term security and forced them to settle for short-term benefits, to the detriment of the former. We note though that this "security" in the case of Mrs Wright would not have been any great sum of money, but would have been better than nothing, and, in Mrs Wright's case, would have helped to improve her self-esteem in the knowledge that she had a small sum of money that was hers to use as she pleased.

Mrs Wright was doing the best that she could given the circumstances of her life. She visited the hypertensive clinic monthly, because her blood pressure was sufficiently high for it to be of concern to her doctors. This was not surprising when one relates this to the worried frown that she wore constantly and to her disclosure that she worried all the time. Her arthritis was very painful at times and she needed to be on medication to alleviate her suffering. She had no money to buy medication, and received most of what she needed from the health centre close to her home.

She stated that she was depressed, and looked depressed: head hung low and shoulders slouched forward. She stated that she lived from day to day, and worried about the future. She had this to say about her diet, "I think I'm so thin because I have not been eating properly because I cannot afford to do any better." On one occasion when I visited her it was about four in the afternoon. She remarked that she had only had a small breakfast and was hungry at the time. She was worrying that her son who lived at the house was planning to move out to live with his girlfriend. She would then be left completely without financial assistance if he stopped contributing, as she suspected he would if he no longer lived at the house.

Mrs Wright's situation was not unique and would have been similar to the life situation of some of the more unfortunate women of this age group, although perhaps not a large percentage. These were women who had given a life of service to husband, children and community, but who found that in their old age they had become ill and had very limited resources to cope with their life situations.

The next case shows a woman whose life situation afforded her a more conducive environment in which to manage her life and her health, and take advantage of the available health services.

Case No. 12

Mrs Thomas was fifty-six years old and worked as a cleaner at the local college. She was not legally married but had lived with her common-law husband for the past thirty years. He was the father of her six children and she had been in a visiting relationship with him for ten years while she still lived in the home of an aunt who had adopted her as a child. She remarked that although she and her partner were not legally married they had lived a happier life than many married couples. Her children, three male and three female, ranged in age from twenty-seven to thirty-nine years.

Mrs Thomas and her husband owned their house and shared it with their youngest daughter and her three children. That daughter had returned home to live when her relationship with her common-law husband had broken down.

Mrs Thomas was a calm, quiet woman who apparently had been very resourceful all her adult life and had found ways of making additional sums of money to supplement whatever she and her husband had earned jointly from their regular employment. Her husband had worked for many years as a hospital porter, but had lost his job during the restructuring of the health sector in the mid-1980s.[17] At that point, Mrs Thomas decided that her family should establish a small shop at her house, which would be operated by her husband. This they did, selling basic food items, sweets and ice to their neighbours. "We do not make a lot of profit, but it gives my husband something to do," she said.

No one would guess from Mrs Thomas's apparent energy and resourcefulness that she was not in perfect health. She informed me quite casually that she was hypertensive and diabetic, and that she had had a mastectomy five years previously for cancer of the breast. She remarked, however, that she was in good spirits and had returned to work within a few months of the surgery.

She stated that the main difference her cancer surgery had made to her life was that at the end of her workday, she did not have the energy she had previously to do a great deal of housework at home, so she was glad that her daughter had returned home. Her daughter was not employed, so while she went out to work, her daughter stayed at home and did all the housework. She stated that she had a good relationship with her daughter. She said she was not worried about the future because of the good relationship that she had with this daughter. She added that she also had a good relationship with her daughter-in-law.

Here was a woman at midlife who was not in perfect health but who, because of the reality of domestic relations, was obliged to continue to work outside the home. She appeared comfortable with her situation. She was recovering from breast surgery, but instead of staying out of the workforce, she recognized her responsibilities towards her family and continued working. Clearly, she did not recognize that she had the freedom to be ill. However, such was the discourse that surrounded her life that she responded by being a truly "disciplined body", as Foucault described, insomuch that she appeared quite happy to be out at work. She did not do this out of the sense of being a martyr, but genuinely appeared to enjoy going out to work, and meeting the other cleaners and having conversations with the college students. At the same time she encouraged and advised her husband about what could be done to improve the little shop that they owned. She was a good example of how many women of this age group operated. They recognized what had to be done, and set about achieving it.

WOMEN AS PROVIDERS OF HEALTH CARE

With reference to health and women of this age group, an important point that has to be made is that women of this age group spend a great deal of their working day taking responsibility for the health care of family and community members; this type of behaviour is expected of older women, and rarely is anyone else allocated this responsibility. There were those informal situations in which women gave advice about cough remedies, treatments for fever, worms and so on to their grandchildren. But there were other situations in which women were much more actively involved in the health of family and community.

The data collected revealed that 7 per cent of the working-class sample and 12 per cent of the middle-class sample were actively engaged at the time of the study in almost full-time health care of a spouse, elderly parent or sibling. For example, Mrs Green, a Hope Pastures woman, lived with her sixty-five-year-old husband and her ninety-year-old mother. There were others who, like Mrs Ulett (Case no. 1), cared for at least one elderly person within the community; Mrs Ulett provided care for an elderly woman until she was hospitalized. This excerpt from Case no. 1 reveals how women like Mrs Ulett are expected to take responsibility for the health care of older community members, but are only grudgingly provided with the resources (and in insufficient quantity) to do the job.

Mrs Ulett felt it an affront to have to make a special request to the elderly woman's son to reimburse the expenses she incurred in the care of the elderly lady.

This situation of providing care without the necessary support was not uncommon, and the women who were left to do these tasks continued with them because of their sense of community, as they realized that there was a job to be done, and that there were not too many others around who were prepared to do it.

We could argue that in their interactions with the health service, older women had "power" to demand health care for themselves and family members in their charge. They also had power to go to those places where health care was available. What they did not have power to do, however, was to ensure that they would always gain access to the service or be able to pay for such service and related expenses, such as prescriptions.

The following quotations from these women were typical of what they had to say about the availability of service and the cost. "Sometimes we have to wait a very long time in the clinics for service, and if we need to go to the public hospital, then we might even have to wait longer to be served." Another complained about the high cost of medication. She said, "Sometimes I do not take all my medicine because the medicine costs too much, and I want the tablets to last a longer period." Another woman complained that her medication cost J$5 per tablet and she had to take three tablets per day, everyday.

It was clear from listening to these older women that the power of the governmental health authorities was important in relation to these women's dissatisfaction with the health care that was available to them. One might also argue that they were not alone in this, as the constraints on the national budget during the period under consideration allowed for only so much to be allocated to health. We note from chapter 1 that resources allocated to health care was inadequate, and midlife and older women were forced to compete with all other age groups for benefits within the health service.

CONCLUSION

Women get to this stage of life in good or bad health depending on the kind of life they have lived, the amount of stress in their lives, the kind of diet to which they had access and the kind of health care that had been available to them many years previously. We would expect to find that there would have been significant differences in the health status of these women based on their class position. However, the working-class women, apart from a few exceptions, were not significantly worse off. These findings affirm that the women in the study had spent many years in a Jamaican society that had been under less pressure, in terms of the economic provisions and the availability of health care, than existed in 1990–91. The women were in reasonably good health because they had benefited from a Jamaica which had seen better days.

In terms of overall health, almost all of the women complained that not enough had been done for the health of women of their age group, and gave many suggestions as to what else could have been done by the government to ensure the maintenance of the health of women of their group. The most frequent complaint to surface across the two groups was the high cost of health care and especially the high cost of medication. Those who lived in the working-class community were particularly pleased that they were often able to obtain their medication at a specially reduced price, and stated that they would not otherwise have been able to afford the cost of the required medicines.

As long as women had functional health they declared that they felt well. It did not seem to matter to them that they had to take medication for hypertension or arthritic pains. As long as that was "all" and they could keep on moving, then they were well. There was not one woman in the study from whom one gained the impression that she was a hypochondriac. Even those who had serious illness were still willing to continue to do for their families over and above what their doctors thought fit. They understood discursively, that is, as a result of the totality of their cultural experience, what had to be done. But this was perhaps just as well, as their relatives did not encourage them to adopt the sick role.[18]

These women did not even really have any serious complaints about the health services. They realized its inadequacies and had many suggestions as to what else might be done but did not have unrealistic expectations as to what could actually be done within this service for them. They realized that they were not treated as a special group, and that it was highly unlikely that they would be, given the known limitations of the public health-care system. Some had access in their community to a clinic for treatment of hypertension, but there was nothing as far as they were concerned that dealt with the whole person, from the social, to the emotional, to the physically ill, in an integrated fashion. It was for this reason that some complained that there was no service that enabled them to learn about the change of life, for example. They felt that this was the kind of additional service

Midlife and Older Women

that could be provided and which would do well to encourage women to feel better about themselves and be more empowered at this stage of their lives.

Within the discourse of health, women of this age group were not constituted as a special group in need of health care, but were constituted as health-care givers for family and community. They lived their lives accordingly, using whatever power they had to maintain their health and to gain access to some amount of health care for themselves.

A great deal of what we have learnt here about the lives of Jamaican midlife and older women was that there was a fair amount of confusion in the discourses that were presented about their health and their life situation in general. This confusion arose largely because the discourses exclude the voices of women of this age group. It was clear that these women had their own discourses, but no forum in which to present them. Consequently, what they know about themselves, about their health and the care they provide to others is still largely a repressed discourse.

CHAPTER 5
COPING WITH WIDOWHOOD

> I miss my husband as I had grown accustomed to taking care of him over the past two years when I had retired from work and he had been ill at home.
> — *Interview with Respondent no. 11*

> I never knew what he did with his money and there was only a little which I ever got my hands on. I know how to control money and use it wisely. I am now better off financially.
> — *Interview with Respondent no. 33*

INTRODUCTION

In this chapter, an attempt is made to unravel what widowhood meant to the women of the two communities and to discover what changes took place in their lives as a result of widowhood; what freedoms they gained, what levels of independence they were able to achieve and what controls were placed on them by family and community, with regard to everyday living and especially in relation to expressions of their sexuality. Because widowhood leaves some women in

a vulnerable economic situation, it was important to know how they fared economically, in relation to the provisions they made for themselves and the benefits
they received from the state, either on their own behalf or as a result of the
contributions that had been paid by their husbands. In this regard, the chapter
explores the informal and formal supports that are available to widows, and case
studies are presented to clarify and provide examples about particular situations
in the lives of these women.

Although most women do not look forward to widowhood, it is invariably
the reality for the majority of married women as they grow older in Jamaica. In
Jamaica, women are far more likely to be widowed than are men (Rawlins 1989a).
Overall, higher male mortality rates explain why there are more women than men
who are widowed.[1] Another contributor to a greater number of widowed women
is the difference in life expectancy; for Jamaica it was 72.6 years for women and
68.1 years for men in 1982.[2] Men also usually marry women younger than themselves and then predecease them, thus adding to the pool of widows. Additionally,
in those relatively rare instances where men are predeceased by their wives, many
will remarry, thus removing themselves from the category of the widowed.

A widow is defined here as a woman whose husband has predeceased her.
This definition excludes women whose common-law partners lived with them until
the time of their death and only includes women who were legally married and
whose spouse had died.[3] In Jamaica, widows represent a significant proportion of
the population. The national census of Jamaica for 1982 indicates that there were
37,644 widows in a population of 693,741 women in the age group fifteen years
old and over. The data imply that one out of eighteen adult females over the age of
eighteen years was a widow, and here common-law widows were also excluded.

Widowhood and gender relations, I shall argue, are different in Jamaica from
those that are reported in the literature for North America and Europe (Lopata
1986; Phillipson 1980; Carr et al. 2001; Utz et al. 2002). In these countries, where
many women do not return to work when they marry, their relations with their
husbands will of necessity be different from the situation that obtains in Jamaica,
where working mothers are the norm. Consequently, in Jamaica, and indeed in
other parts of the Caribbean, the responses of women and their relatives to widowhood will be quite different from the responses of persons who have lived their
lives with a partner who was essentially the primary provider. In situations where
the husband is the primary provider, their wives will have gained their status and

part of their identity largely from their relationship to their husband, the "worker". Naturally, the situation will be different for women whose identity is more closely linked to what they do for themselves outside the home on a daily basis.

This book argues that within Jamaican society there are two main discourses surrounding the lives of widowed women, and that these two discourses are contradictory in some senses. It argues also that in addition to these two discourses there are other factors, social and economic, that impinge greatly on the lives of widowed women. The discourse that most people know suggests that widowhood in Jamaica involves a degree of disorganization similar to that experienced by American women. Lopata (1986) argued that widowhood involves a degree of disorganization at least as strong as that experienced by the male upon retirement, and that women suffer both economically and psychologically as a result of being widowed.

However, this book argues that there is another discourse surrounding widowhood, which was created by the widows themselves, and was different from the dominant discourse. The content of this discourse was not widely known in the society, and I have interpreted it as a form of resistance to the discourse of disorganization. This discourse, articulated by the widows interviewed for this study, may be called the discourse of liberation. For some widows, then, their lives were better after widowhood; they were more independent, they had more freedom, and they were able to make better use of their time than had been the case when they were married. However, some of these women were ambivalent in their responses, in that they also expressed some of the views that were to be found in the discourse of disorganization. At the same time as they celebrated their new autonomy they mourned the loss of companionship and the economic loss.

The issue of widowhood is important in the lives of women of this age group. It usually occurs during midlife or old age, at a time when the woman's children are grown. Widowhood sometimes happens when the woman has left the labour market and is beginning to look forward to a more relaxed and independent time in her life. The issue of widowhood is important in relation to the assumptions of this research, in that it was especially upon being widowed that the lack of a widely accepted discourse of widowhood as liberation enhanced the vulnerability of these women to more widely established norms, which, in effect, circumscribed their freedom. In considering widowhood, a discourse was revealed that was found to be full of power; enabling the alternative lived experience of some widows to be effectively denied or suppressed.

The situation of widowhood in itself allows for many contradictory views and relationships. It is a time when relatives are faced with a dramatic change in a particular woman's situation, being left without a man in her life. It is a time when adult children may have to forge new relationships with their mothers and adult sons might feel they need to guard their mothers against the interest of other men in the community. And it is a time when the women, as well as their relatives and friends, have to face the reality of the dominant discourse with regard to the sexuality of older women in the society. As long as their husbands are alive, there is no need to publicly examine or give thought to sexual intimacy in the lives of these older women. But when their husbands are gone, and they seek new partners or potential partners seek them, then the issue of their sexuality becomes a point of concern, not only for themselves and their potential partners, but also for other members of their family and members of the community. The analysis of the data and the presentation of the case studies reveal how the widows lived their lives despite and within the contradictory discourses on widowhood.

What is this discourse on the sexuality of older women? Rohlehr (1990), in his review "Images of Men and Women in 1930s Calypsos", makes reference to the older woman. Although he looks at Trinidad society, there are some similarities for Jamaica. His review shows that there is no doubt that the older woman sees herself as a sexual being, even if the society would prefer to believe that this is not the case. Not only is she sexually active within her own original family situation, but many of the calypsos make reference to her relationship with the younger man, the proverbial "sweet man", whom no doubt she has come to know after her "spouse" of an age closer to her own has moved on or passed on. The calypsonians condemn the older woman even though she provides materially and emotionally for the "sweet man".

Many of the calypsos suggest that "she", the older woman, is doing something that goes against the widespread norms and we know that, in the Caribbean, a good calypsonian is nothing if not the voice of the people. Calypsonian Lion, mentioned by Rohlehr, makes reference to the sexual voracity of the older woman in his calypso "Ounga": "though she was old she was advantageous /And not a minute of the night she would leave me alone" (Rohlehr 1990, 234). We see from this brief reference to a particular societal understanding of the older woman's sexuality that the society recognizes its presence but also ridicules it.

Another Caribbean writer, C.L.R. James (1981), draws our attention to the concerns of neighbours and relatives about the intimate relationships of older women. In *Minty Alley* his characters question the relationship that the middle-aged Mrs Rouse has with her kept "sweet man", Mr Benoit. All the residents of the yard felt that Mrs Rouse should not be in this relationship. The comments made by her niece, Maisie, summarize some of the sentiments expressed by the other residents of the yard. Maisie says to Mr Haynes, "I often wonder how old people make love. Love is a matter for young people, people like you and me, Mr. Haynes" (James 1981, 31).

WIDOWS IN AUGUST TOWN AND HOPE PASTURES

In the sample of two hundred women of the two communities there was a total of fifty widows.[4] Twenty-four of these were in August Town and twenty-six were in Hope Pastures. Of these all the Hope Pastures women and twenty of the August Town women had been living with their husbands up to the time of their death. A total of twenty-one of these women, mainly the middle-class women (nineteen of them), were employed outside the home in paid employment.

The literature on widowhood (Schlesinger 1980; Morgan 1981; Burkhauser, Holden and Myers 1986) speaks of the negative changes in women's lives occasioned by widowhood; therefore it was necessary for this researcher to begin to explore exactly what changes had occurred in these women's lives. I sought to do this by asking questions about what they saw as the changes in their lives. I also asked if there were any new freedoms that they were experiencing that they had not had while they lived with their husbands.

The Meaning of Widowhood: Ambivalent Emotions

The most important change identified by the combined group was that following the death of a spouse, they were lonely and lacked companionship. When the responses were disaggregated by community it became obvious that this loneliness and lack of companionship was more likely to be the case for the women of Hope Pastures, not surprisingly perhaps, since the middle-class couples "did more" together in their leisure time (see chapter 2). Additionally, more of them (50 per cent) had been living alone with the spouse prior to his demise. On his death they found themselves in a house alone.

The data show that those who had been living in a house alone, away from friends and kin, spoke more of being lonely than those women who had other people living in their homes. There were more people to be found in the homes of the August Town women than there were in Hope Pastures, consequently the passing of the husband would be experienced differently in that, with more people in the home, there would be less need to feel abandoned, dejected and absolutely lonely. Twice as many of the Hope Pastures women as the working-class August Town women reported this loneliness as the main change. The more recent widows were also more likely to comment on their loneliness, as, for example, the fifty-seven-year-old woman who had been widowed for eighteen months, who said, "I feel lonely even in a crowd."

For the August Town women, the main change reported was that life had become harder, by which they meant mainly economically harder, and here, twice as many of them as the women of Hope Pastures stated that this was their situation. Life is generally hard for women in a working-class, low-income community, even with a spouse alive. Throughout their lives most would have been involved in income-earning activities, which would have contributed significantly to the household. That life was reported to be harder reflected the general hardship of their situation, and the impact that the withdrawal of another income, even a relatively small one, had on their lives. Other responses were that there had been no change, and the counter-intuitive, very positive response that they were now free to do as they pleased. Therefore, for the women of the two communities widowhood meant differ-ent things. For the middle-class women of Hope Pastures, the experience was essentially one of loneliness, while for the poor women of August Town, it was a harder life.

Not all the women, however, were overcome by the changes that had occurred in their lives as a result of widowhood. In fact, the August Town women, even those who said life was harder, were not really overwrought. They were perhaps not much worse off than they had been when their husbands were alive. Morgan (1981), in a study of economic change at midlife, noted that many widows were poor prior to widowhood; consequently widowhood was not the major cause of poverty for the group studied. Similarly, the working-class women in this study were already relatively poor, so widowhood could not be cited as the cause of their inadequate economic condition.

Six of these women (12 per cent) found that particular burdens had been removed from their lives with the passing of their husbands and that they were free to do as they liked and to come and go as they pleased. So for at least this 12 per cent, their independence had been realized upon widowhood.

It was important to this research to know what exactly had been some of the changes that had occurred in the lives of these women. They were therefore asked about changes related to their leisure time and to their household responsibilities. More than 50 per cent of the women in each group stated that they now had more time for themselves. They might have been lonely and worse off financially but 62 per cent of the combined group felt they had more time for themselves. This means that the women saw the men as drawing heavily on their time, and they were now able to transfer this time into other activities. This was the case especially in the situation in which the husband had been ill and had been nursed by the wife for a prolonged period.

Two case studies follow. The first is that of a working-class woman from August Town. It shows her situation after she was widowed and notes that she did not feel that she was worse off but that she was better able to use her spare time. The second case study shown below is that of a Hope Pastures widow, who, although she missed her husband initially, did not feel particularly deprived in her new status as a widow.

Case No. 13

Mrs Dill was a very interesting woman who, at sixty-five years old, had been widowed for four years. She and her husband had lived together for thirty years and they had four children, three sons and a daughter. All the children except one daughter had been residing in the United States for nine to ten years. Her husband had been a policeman and had been retired for five years prior to his passing.

During her younger days she had fostered a total of six children: two who were her husband's children from a previous relationship, a niece, a young girl (a distant relative), a non-relative and a grandchild. She had three grandchildren living with her at the time of the interviews. She did not seem overly unhappy about having her grandchildren with her but stated that they took up a great deal of time and sometimes prevented her from doing what she would prefer to do. She did not complain about being lonely, as she had been taking in boarders since her husband passed away. Not only did she have additional company in the house as a result, but her income was supplemented by this, as well as the rental of an apartment at the rear of her home.

She felt that widowhood had given her new freedoms in that she was able to spend more time working for the church and for the poor. She had many responsibilities in the church and headed two committees.

With regard to her financial situation, she felt that she was better off than many working-class widows. She received financial assistance, from her three children in the United States, a police pension of J$200 each month and a widow's pension of J$90 fortnightly. She also felt that she was better off financially than when her husband had been alive as she was a better manager of money, as her husband had been very wasteful. "I never knew what he did with his money and there was only a little which I ever got my hands on. I know how to control money and use it wisely," she said.

She noted that the two pensions together were barely sufficient to pay the water rates and the telephone bill but not the electricity bill, and, like most of the women of August Town, she complained about the high and increasing cost of living.

With regard to establishing a new relationship, she stated that she had no desire to do so, but preferred to use her time teaching young women of the community to sew and to become involved in other community activities.

Above we see a woman who was not unduly worried about having become a widow. Her life had certainly not become any more difficult, despite the new experience. In fact, it would seem that she was at the time better off, as she was able to control the resources that came into her household. So often, but not always with ambivalence, the widows told me that being a widow was in some ways better than being a married woman. It was good to control one's own resources of money and time, to be responsible for one's days. Some women actually had more money, as well as more control of what was available. All this came as a surprise to this researcher, a married woman. These women were giving voice to a repressed or silent discourse. The role of the unhappy widow, of a woman whose fulfilment in life ended with the death of her man, was plainly one that they resisted. Perhaps by asking them a question about "changes", rather than problems, this researcher had made it possible for them to speak. Whatever the explanation, it became clear that at least 12 per cent of the widows in the study experienced some improvement in their lives as a result of widowhood. A woman being better off and in control of her life as a widow was true for some and important to them, and they wanted others to know about it.

The widow referred to below also contributed to my understanding of the repressed societal discourse on widowhood. She stated that after her initial sadness in relation to her husband's demise she concluded that her new situation was not particularly disadvantageous. Her sentiments are similar to those expressed by a number of the other widows.

Case No. 14

Mrs Neil, a very light-skinned woman, had been a widow for sixteen years. Her husband had been an insurance broker and they had been married for thirty years. She was the mother of three children, one son and two daughters, but one daughter had died in a motor vehicle accident fifteen years previously. Her other two children were forty-five and forty-two years old at the time of the interviews. She had a total of four grandchildren and was very proud of her offspring and their children. Her son had been living in the United States since the late 1970s. Mrs Neil had also obtained US citizenship and visited the United States frequently.

Her daughter had been twice married and twice divorced, and, at the time of the interviews, she and her daughter lived with Mrs Neil. She said, "This is not the life I wished for my daughter, but now I can see that it is working out with some advantage on both sides. My daughter after a lot of distress now has a fairly safe home here with me. She does not pay rent as I have a very large house here by myself. I am able to keep an eye on the granddaughter sometimes. She is eight years old and is good company, so although I am widowed I am not lonely. My daughter also pays her way, so I have some financial assistance from her. Not that this is really necessary as I had worked as a dress designer all of my working life and have made quite a bit of money. I had saved my money and made some investments and my husband had also left me well taken care of. I also have my own house. My son abroad would help out if it ever became necessary."

She was happy that she and her husband invested in a home when they did. The mortgage had been paid off and she had some savings. Her economic situation, she said, was satisfactory and her daughter who lived with her helped her to meet her financial responsibilities. Her son in the United States was also helpful to her and she visited him fairly frequently.

At age seventy Mrs Neil was a very active and well-organized woman. She was very creative, had many talents and was anxious to share her skills with other people. From the discussion with her I realized that she was a philanthropist of sorts. She taught her skills to young women who came under her influence, including women who had worked for her as domestic helpers.

About her sexuality, she said, "I feel satisfied with myself, but since my husband's death I have lost all interest in sexual matters." She said she had no desire to remarry, out of respect for her children, especially her son. She said, "I had a lovely husband and wanted to leave it at that. Also I did not feel the sex urge any more."

She received neither widow's pension nor NIS pension, although she had contributed to the NIS. Actually she should have received an NIS pension as she had been employed for decades, but she had not bothered to make a claim.

Although she looked well, Mrs Neil said her health was bad. She had suffered from headaches since childhood and the doctors had not been able to cure them. She took medication, which had a number of troublesome side effects. Like many of the other middle-class women in this study, she had had a hysterectomy. She had a stomach ulcer. She believed that older women should visit their doctor annually, but did not always follow her belief because of the prohibitive costs.

Mrs Neil's life was one that fitted perfectly with the ambivalence of the two main discourses on widowhood. Her economic situation had not deteriorated as a result of her status as a widow; she was not lonely because she had taken her daughter and granddaughter into her home to share the house with her and she most certainly used her leisure time well. I shall return to the point of her loss of interest in sexual matters and her fear of losing the respect of her children. The experience of many widows suggested that when marriage ends, the discourse of the inappropriateness of sexual activity for older women (see also chapter 2) is accepted by the widows themselves, who differ in this respect from their still-married peers.

Change in Household Responsibilities

Some of the women made reference to "changes" in their household responsibilities. It is interesting that both groups saw themselves as having fewer household responsibilities after their husbands had passed away, although the Hope Pastures women noticed a reduction in their domestic workload more frequently than the August Town women (50 per cent and 30 per cent, respectively). This statement, when linked with their responses about their leisure time, indicates the amount of time these midlife and older women devoted to the care of husbands and the home.

The comments made by the women were in relation to their reduced household responsibilities and included statements such as:

"I only cook three times a week now. Sometimes I don't cook at all."
"I have very little heavy washing to do."
"It is much easier to keep the house tidy."

Apart from the occasional feeling of loneliness, most of these women were glad to have reclaimed their time, and were finding things to do to fill the hours that previously had been devoted to housework. One Hope Pastures woman, who is described in the case study that follows, was doing things she had wanted to do for four decades. She had discontinued piano lessons when she married. She had settled down and had seven children. After nine years as a widow, and having recovered from her grief over her husband's death, for the first time in forty years she finally had time to return to the piano lessons she had given up as a young woman, and she was absolutely delighted that she was able to do this.

Case No. 15

Mrs Carr was sixty-five years old and had been a widow for nine years. Her husband had been an accountant. She had married at a very early age by Jamaican standards, when she was nineteen, and had seven children over an eighteen-year period. Two of her children were health professionals who lived in the United States. A third child also lived in the United States and the other four lived with their families in Jamaica.

Earlier on in her middle years she had been responsible for the care of the three children of her youngest daughter. Mrs Carr's husband had died during that period when life had already become quite stressful and the three children stayed with her for a further four years before joining their mother in the United States. She said, "Now life is considerably less stressful and all the children have been very helpful. They give me gifts and other assistance although I do not really need to take things from them. I have my own income and work when I feel like it." Although she was a widow and said she missed her husband greatly when he passed away, she also stated that she had become very independent. Reflecting on her status as a widow, she said, "It took me three years to get over my bereavement, but now I am fine. I miss the companionship of my husband as I don't like to be in this house by myself, and it is for that reason that I now have a boarder and a tenant in my home, who provides an additional income of J$1,000 and J$3,000 per month, respectively."

Mrs Carr lived in a very well-appointed house by Hope Pastures standards. She was satisfied with her life, her economic situation and the way her children had turned out. She attributed the relative success of her children to the fact that she was a very strict disciplinarian and that her children received the education they required. On the issue of remarriage she had this to say: "I have not remarried because I am more independent than most of the men I meet. Unless the prospective husband could give me a nice house I would not consider it. I could not give up what I have to get less as my children would look down on me. I have seven children and their spouses to take care of me. If I remarry I would have only one person. So I'm already better off. I'm enjoying my life. I have a lot of spare time on my hands and I have decided to return to piano lessons. I played the piano before I had children."

New Freedom

The questionnaire had given the widows the opportunity to talk about new freedoms: the freedom to participate in activities that they would not previously have been able to do. More than a third of the entire group reported that they had these new freedoms, but there was a slightly higher percentage of middle-class widows (42 per cent) who stated that they had these new freedoms, compared to 33 per cent for the working-class community.

These women appeared very pleased with their new freedoms, and the list of activities they provided tells us something of the nature of the relationships they had with their spouses and perhaps about the issues that might have led to disagreements between them. The most important freedom referred to was that of "going to church when I want". This suggests that these women in the past had desired to spend more time in religious activities, but had either been prevented from doing so by their husbands or had refrained from fuller participation because of the conflict they expected in relation to their involvement in an activity that their husbands did not feel as strongly positive about as they did. Being able to spend more time in church was more frequently stated by the August Town sample (20 per cent compared to 4 per cent of the middle-class sample), which might suggest that their spouses had been more averse to their church activities than were the spouses of the Hope Pastures sample.

The second most important freedom mentioned by the women was that they were now able to "come and go" as they pleased. This suggests that during their lives as women with husbands, there were times when they perceived that they were restricted in their need to be away from the home, because their husbands required that they should be there, or that their husbands would question their need to be elsewhere. The women of the Hope Pastures sample more frequently cited the importance of coming and going as they pleased (15 per cent compared to 4 per cent of the August Town sample). This suggests that the Hope Pastures sample had activities outside the home, which in the past they had forgone in order to be available to do things around the home or for their husbands. On being widowed they became aware that they had time to undertake those activities. It could be that while their husbands were alive, they had desired involvement in these activities that they now have the freedom to do, but of themselves felt no need for the participation because they had their husband as company. Conversely, it could be that their husbands actively prevented them from participating, a situation that could have led to resentments and conflicts, and explain the apparently joyous remarks of this minority of women about their new freedoms.

Surprisingly, more than a third of the women spoke of this new freedom. However, almost two-thirds reported no such experience, even though many had reported positive changes. This suggests that many of them were not thinking of these positive changes as "new freedoms". My question to them was too specific to tap into their way of thinking, in part, I suggest, because their alternative discourse about the benefits of widowhood was not fully formulated, but rather, like all repressed discourses, existed in a more or less inchoate state. They could respond positively to an open concept like "change", but not to a narrow pre-definition of "new freedoms".

The case that follows has many similarities to the situation of other women interviewed but highlights the ambivalence in the women's reactions to their widowhood. We see a woman who missed her husband. We also see a woman who was very resourceful and had become very independent. This woman, like other women who had been widowed, was left to fend for herself by the society and was neglected by the friends of her late husband. Like many other widows, she was no longer invited to social functions to which she would normally have been invited prior to her husband's death. It was in this type of situation that we were able to see demonstrated the difficulties family, friends and community had coping with women who were no longer "attached" to a man. Here was the "manless" woman, an unplaceable person in many social settings.

The case gives some examples of the ambivalence in the discourse surrounding widowhood and one woman's experienced reality.

Case No. 16

Mrs Lindo at sixty-three years old was an interesting and articulate woman. She had been married to a medical doctor for twenty-three years and they had three children. She had been widowed for sixteen years and the children ranged in age from sixteen to twenty-one years at the time she became a widow. The oldest child, an engineer, was unmarried and lived with her. He helped her with the shopping and house maintenance and she did his housekeeping. He also provided her with what she described as "a significant sum of money which takes care of all the bills related to the management of the house".

Of her children she had this to say: "I have an excellent relationship with them. One lives abroad and he frequently sends gifts and money." Prior to being widowed she had not worked out of the house apart from a brief stint as a clerk early in her marriage, before the birth of her children. On widowhood she was faced with the responsibility of ensuring the tertiary education of her three children, and despite the provisions that had been made by her husband, she found it necessary from a financial standpoint to seek employment. She said she thoroughly enjoyed her work, and felt she had "done well by her children".

She complained bitterly about the high cost of living but said that she coped reasonably well although she was underpaid in her job. She owned a second house, which needed some repairs, but once that was done she planned to rent it, so she could increase her income.

She said that widowhood left her very lonely in the early years, especially as she had come from another island and had no relatives in the Kingston area. "A great feeling of loneliness" was the main feeling that she said she had. She also said it was necessary to be strong as a widow, as "it leaves one on one's own". In that regard, she stated that some of her husband's friends and former colleagues had deliberately sidelined her, and after his death she received no further invitations to social functions of the type she had previously attended with her husband. However, she saw some of what had happened to her since that time as positive, in that it had forced her to become more self-reliant. She also added that it was a positive feeling not to have to rush home from work or explain to anyone where she had been.

With regard to benefits she said she had received a life insurance (lump sum) benefit but no personal benefits as her husband had been self-employed and had not paid into a pension scheme.

Problems Associated with Being Widowed

Widowhood had brought some improvements into some of the women's lives, but naturally this was not the case for all the women. Ten of the twenty-four August Town women (42 per cent) and eighteen of the twenty-six Hope Pastures women (68 per cent) said it had brought a set of problems they had not experienced while their husbands had been alive. The main problems that the women mentioned were loneliness and financial difficulties.[5]

Some of those who did not complain about loneliness had sisters, brothers, mothers and children, who either lived with them or had helped them during the early period of their bereavement and continued to help them over the years.[6] Those who helped during the earliest period of their bereavement, the period in which the women stated that they needed the greatest emotional help, included children, sisters, mothers, a wide range of other relatives and friends and former friends and colleagues of their late husbands.

In keeping with theories in the North American literature about how women's lives change on widowhood (Lopata 1986; Zick and Smith 1986; Patterson 1996), this research sought to understand if the widows in the sample had experienced any restrictions in their lives as a result of being widowed, specifically with regard to whether they felt that new controls had been placed on their lives, either by the women themselves or by others in the society, such as their children or other family members. This was one way of trying to determine "change" in the lives of these women. Fifty-four per cent of the combined group of widows stated that there were no restrictions in their lives as a result of their being widowed. However, nine women (18 per cent of the total), one of whom was from August Town and the others, middle-class women from Hope Pastures, felt that their social life had changed. For middle-class women like Mrs Lindo (Case no. 16), life changed drastically, in that their social life had been considerably scaled down.

They stated, for instance, that they rarely went to social functions in the evenings as they were unwilling and sometimes afraid to go out unescorted. These Hope Pastures women had been accustomed to going out socially and were no longer comfortable doing so. Not only were they not comfortable, but in many instances they no longer received invitations, which previously had come in association with their husband's employment or through other organizations to which he belonged. Being excluded socially was an issue that was raised by five of the Hope Pastures women; they were very resentful of the neglect, which they felt had been deliberate on the part of former friends of their husbands. Their exclusion from some of the social functions can be interpreted as their former friends' attempts, even if subconscious, to ensure that these women conformed to what society expected to be their fate. They would be lonely, but at the same time unable to mix with persons with whom they might express their sexuality. At any rate, this was in part the outcome. Naturally, there would have been other reasons why they were not invited, for example, that only couples were invited or because those issuing the invitations did not want to have to ask someone to escort such women home at the end of the function.

Forming New Relationships

Jamaican women rarely remarry after widowhood,[7] but if the women of this study are representative of widowed Jamaican women, only a few become involved in romantic relationships. This is especially the case if they are widowed after the age of fifty years. In this survey, of the fifty widowed women interviewed only four women, two from each community, stated that they had established new relationships after their husbands died. Those who had not formed, or attempted to form, new relationships gave a number of reasons for not doing so, which included: that they had no need for a person any more, that they might lose the respect of their children, that men could not be trusted and that they felt no need to take on such responsibilities any more. This was the situation described by the woman in Case no. 8, in chapter 3. She had this to say about forming new relationships: "I have had a number of offers of sexual friendships from younger men, and men older than myself. They all tell me how attractive I am and that I am letting myself go to waste. But after my husband died, 'that was it' and I did not need that kind of relationship any more." Women were indeed lonely on widowhood, and they did complain about being lonely, especially those who were more recently widowed. But even those who were lonely did not seek to establish new romantic relationships and in fact rejected the advances that were made to them. However, they did not all stay lonely, and some established friendships with other people and found activities in which they could become involved to reduce their feelings of loneliness and depression.

It is interesting that the women stated that they did not form new relationships, although the cases studies are replete with statements about the advances that the women received from men of all ages. The working-class women did not speak of proposals for marriage, but five women made reference to propositions for the formation of new romantic relationships. These August Town women, however, were the ones who most vehemently rejected these advances, as they felt that they and their children might be taken advantage of by these men. They said, for example,

"I did not think I would find a faithful partner."
"Maybe he would be worse than my first husband."
"I did not want to take a man who might have abused my daughter."

Six of the middle-class women stated that they had had marriage proposals and other invitations to become romantically involved. Respondent no. 129, a woman of independent means, who was sixty-five years old and had been widowed at age fifty-six, stated, "I had offers for marriage, but they were not satisfactory. One man, a justice of the peace, wanted me to marry him and leave Kingston to live in St Thomas [a rural parish] and raise chickens." Respondent no. 167, who at age seventy had been widowed for two years, said, "I had two offers of marriage, but I'm really not interested. No one could replace my husband." Another respondent (no. 109) said, "I had one offer of marriage, but I laughed it off. No, no, I really would not do that." Respondent no. 116, who worked as a senior administrator in an educational institution, had been widowed at age fifty-three, and sixteen years later had this to say, "I had a couple of offers, shortly after my husband's passing, but I was not ready to think of it then, and by the time I was ready they had lost interest." Respondent no. 188 stated that she had been propositioned by several married men, but disregarded their attention because of the confusion that kind of relationship could bring to one's life. She had been widowed at age fifty-three and worked as a clerk in a business in Kingston. The study reveals that the majority of the widows who had been propositioned rejected the advances made to them by men and continued to live their lives without partners.

Their responses are interesting in that they said, for example, "I did not need the responsibility", and "I don't need anyone who might eat me down."[8] These were the main comments and, taken all together, the comments reflect these women's negative feelings toward men. Their attitudes undoubtedly speak volumes about the nature of the relationship these women must have had with their husbands, which had led them to this point of mistrust of all men. There were, of course, those few women who stated that theirs had been the ideal marriage and so they were satisfied to keep those memories, and desired no new relationships.

The statement "He might eat me down" is not to be taken lightly. It means that the women were scared that the men might show interest in them in order to take advantage of whatever material resources they had managed to secure for themselves, or whatever had been left them by their husbands. Twenty-one per cent of the working-class women of this study expressed this reservation.

It is interesting that the stronger statements, in this regard, were made by the lower-income women. However, the case studies capture the Hope Pastures women also making similar statements with regard to their resources. The Hope Pastures women were adamant that they were not prepared to share the resources that had been left to them by their spouses with any man who might come court-ing. One reasonably wealthy woman of the Hope Pastures sample was resolute that any such man would need to sign a prenuptial agreement as she planned to leave her property to her children. Other Hope Pastures women in the case studies stated that they were not prepared to entertain any men who were not in a posi-tion to keep them in the fashion to which they were accustomed, and they were not inclined to have men move into the homes their husbands had left them. One woman actually had this to say, "He at least would need to have his own home into which we could move."

Another important reason some women gave for not entering into new relationships was that they were afraid to lose respect, that is the respect of their children first and also the respect of their community. Women were aware that there was a certain policing of their activities; that they were being watched by family and community. Four women in the case studies confided that but for the children they would have established new relationships, but they felt that the children would not have understood. They also did not want to create a situation in which conflict might arise between them and their children because there was a new person in their life. For most women after widowhood, the relationship that they had with their children was important; for some it was more important than any relationship that they thought it might be possible to establish with a new partner. One particular reason, "not wanting anyone", alluding specifically to sexual needs, was the response given by 46 per cent of the Hope Pastures widows, whereas only 5 per cent of the August Town widows gave that response. [9]

Government Benefits and Pensions and Other Support

An important part of this research hinged on the support, formal and informal, these widows received. Forty-two per cent (twenty-one women) were still gainfully employed, but very few received salaries that would have made them contented in their efforts to manage financially, given the economic situation of Jamaica in 1990–91. The dominant discourse included assumptions of some level of support for widows from relatives, friends and the state, and might have influenced the type of assistance received by these women from family and state. The underlying belief that the family takes care of older women has been raised in previous chapters, and we see here that this assumption might have contributed to the neglect widowed women experienced at the hands of the state.

Assistance from Relatives and Friends

Relatives and friends within Jamaica and the Caribbean offer a variety of types of assistance during the early period of the widow's bereavement. However, the question must be asked: how many are likely to continue to provide support to the widow for years after her husband has passed away? The survey sought to explore the nature of the relationships that widows continued to experience with relatives. Fifty per cent (twelve widows) of the August Town group and twenty-one (80 per cent) of the Hope Pastures group admitted that different types of assistance had continued over the years. This included women who had been widowed for more than sixteen years. The data revealed that 33 per cent of the working-class women and only 8 per cent of the middle-class women stated that they received no assistance from their relatives.

Children outnumbered all those who helped during the initial period of the bereavement. This might be taken as evidence for the common societal belief that mothers help their children, who in turn will also help them. The data collected here revealed that women received help from a combination of sources, including their daughters, sisters, mothers, nieces, cousins and a wide range of in-laws. All the widows had received help from at least one source. The findings in this study were in keeping with those of Sanchez (1989), who refers to the work of Town-shend (1965), Blenkner (1965) and Horowitz (1982). These researchers concur on this reciprocity and Sanchez notes, "It has been found that reciprocity or mutual aid is a crucial dimension in relations between the elderly and their children: Aid flows in both directions and may consist of helping with shopping, housework, child care, advice, information exchange, moral support and presents or money" (p. 267). More recent studies also make reference to social support from varied sources (Kanachi, Jones and Galbraith 1996; Byles, Feldman and Mishra 1999; Glaser and Tomassini 2000).

There were a few instances in which these women also claimed to have been helped by their mothers. Bankoff (1983, 229) notes that aged parents (mainly mothers) were important in terms of social support to widowed daughters. She argues that this support was critical to the psychological well-being of the widows in her Chicago study. "Not only were the mothers able to provide 'nurturance', that is, empathy and strong emotional support, but these widowed mothers were able to fully understand their grieving daughters, having experienced the pain and loss themselves."

Those widows who were likely to fare best in terms of informal financial and material support were those who had relatives abroad. Relatives abroad were an important source of financial support, while relatives and friends locally could be depended on more for emotional and practical support.

The family was not the only group that provided assistance to widowed women. Ten working-class women of August Town, which represented 42 per cent of that group, and twenty-one Hope Pastures women (80 per cent of that group) stated that they had received emotional support and financial assistance from friends, especially in the early years of being widowed. Such support included doing odd jobs around the house, providing companionship, shopping and trans-portation. We must note that some of those who gave assistance already lived in these women's homes or came to live with them subsequently, and that this help was not one-sided but reciprocal.

In this study the average wage earned by the working-class women in 1990–91 was J$600 per month, while the average monthly wage for the middle-class women was J$2,300 per month. It was therefore necessary for some of the women to have other types of financial support, whether it was from their children or from other relatives, or from benefits from the state through the NIS, as a pension or a widow's benefit.

State Provisions

In 1990–91 there were state provisions through the NIS for older women and widowed women. The benefits of concern were the old-age benefit, which becomes available on retirement, and the widow's benefit. The old-age benefit was particularly important because approximately one half of the women of this study qualified for it either in their own right as women who had retired or as widows.

Another benefit for which some of the widows in this study were eligible was the old-age grant. Those women who did not satisfy the necessary conditions for a pension should have been eligible to receive a grant, provided that they had made fifty-two weekly contributions to the NIS.[10] The widow's benefit was also a benefit for which some of these widows qualified. Women became eligible for widow's benefit upon the death of their husband or their partner in a common-law union. To qualify for widow's benefit the widow was required to satisfy specific conditions relating to her age, the duration of her marital union and whether or not she had minor children.[11]

Pensions and widow's benefits were seen to be inadequate. The women all complained that these benefits, which either they or their husbands had contributed to in good faith, were inadequate when the time came for the benefits to be paid, and that these benefits did not afford the type of protection they had anticipated when they had agreed or had been co-opted into the schemes.

In 1991, the NIS benefits were adequate only to help to maintain the standard of living of those who had contributed, and those whose husbands had contributed. Consequently, women who had worked for a large part of their years in the informal sector and who had not contributed meaningfully to the NIS found that there was little for them to get from the system. Most of the low-income women in this survey who received a pension in 1990–91 received approximately J$88 (US$20) every other week.[12]

The widows in this study ranged in age from fifty to seventy-four years. Most had been employed out of the home during their adult years and twenty-one (two from August Town and nineteen from Hope Pastures) were currently employed. The 50 per cent (mainly middle-class widows) who had worked formally had paid into the NIS, and if their husbands had worked formally, they too would have paid into the government pension scheme, thus enabling their wives to benefit from their pensions and the widow's benefit.

Thirty-eight per cent of these women, nine from August Town and ten from Hope Pastures, received no benefits from the government after they were widowed, while a total of twenty-four women or 48 per cent (nine from August Town and fifteen from Hope Pastures) received benefits. The differences were statistically significant by community. More of the Hope Pastures women, whose husbands had been middle-class, employed men, received government pensions and other benefits. Most of those who received the benefits complained that they were grossly inadequate and made comments about what other benefits they thought should be available to widows. The question that was asked was: What other benefits do you think should be available? The working-class women stated that the pensions should be considerably increased, that a medical scheme should be available to all pensioners as they were unable to pay medical costs with a limited pension and some felt that there should be a pension for those persons who had been self-employed and had not paid into the NIS. They felt that this situation had arisen because those self-employed workers had not been aware that they could have contributed to the NIS on their own behalf.

The middle-class women were adamant that there was a need for the pensions to be significantly increased. The following comment by one woman summarizes the sentiments of the group: "It is ridiculous what we get as a pension, especially when our husbands had been professional workers and had served the government for decades." Other comments referred to their need to get a double pension, that is the pension of their husband as well as their own widow's pension.

Taken all together, the women of the two groups saw benefits as inadequate and in need of considerable increases. There was, however, a certain cynicism in a small number in each group who felt that it would not help for the widows to look to the government for increased benefits as the government was unlikely to do much more for older women. The women of the working-class community, however, stated that the benefits were small and had stayed small because midlife and older women were not militant and would be too embarrassed to demonstrate in the street like nurses and teachers had done in 1991 for an improvement in their wages and conditions. The women in reality accepted parts of the dominant discourse of widowhood, which saw militancy as out of character for themselves, and consequently opted not to use such methods to attempt to improve their situation; the voices of the few braver widows were "quietened".

The worsening economic conditions of Jamaica in 1990–91, with inflation and the resultant high cost of living, made it extremely difficult for these widows to survive financially. Those who had depended solely on their husband's income were in a desperate situation. For these widows, the widow's benefit or the pension was less than their husbands had received as salary. Everyone was certainly going to be worse off financially if the pension or widow's benefit was to be matched against a wage, no matter how small that wage would have been. Even if it had been large enough and consistent enough to warrant entry into the NIS scheme or the other benefits schemes, the widow would certainly be worse off economically.

CONCLUSION

Widowhood, although an experience few of the women relished, was one which, despite bringing loneliness and hardships, enabled some women to become more resourceful and to experience a new pleasure in being in control of both their financial situation and their time. For each the experience had been different. For the more recently widowed the situation was in some instances still traumatic, and one those widows continued to express as a great loss. For some, there was a real ambivalence in their experience as widows and no alternate discourse in which to express both their loss and their freedom.

The women generally, and especially those of August Town, seemed to have recovered from the negative aspects of their widowhood experience and were getting on with their lives as best they could. Widowhood to them did not appear nearly as burdensome as it appears in the known discourses of widowhood. The explanation this research offers is that Jamaican and Caribbean women are different from the women who are generally referenced in the literature, in three main ways. First, family life is organized differently; second, their work lives and the amount of time they spend in the labour force over the various stages of their life cycles are different; and third, the ways they relate to their husbands are different in that they are income earners themselves and do not see themselves as dependent only on their spouses. Additionally, in some instances, the women in the study were better able to reorganize themselves after widowhood than would have been the case for women who had no contacts outside the home and little understanding of the operations of the public sphere.

We note that 30 per cent of all the widows stated that they were lonely. Two-thirds of these were middle-class women who had been living alone with their spouses. The others did not experience loneliness the way women in some of the literature reviewed did (Lopata 1979; Zick and Smith 1986; Murdock et al. 1998; Carr et al. 2001), because of their experience of sharing their homes with their relatives and because they tended to share few activities with their husbands anyway. The phenomenon of house sharing has long been the case among low-income families and is now becoming increasingly common among middle-income families. These women knew what was expected of them by family and society, and behaved accordingly. The people with whom they shared were in many ways as important to the women's lives as were their husbands, and these women focused on them, and in many ways lived their lives with these relatives uppermost in their minds.

Lopata (1973), Zick and Smith (1988) and Patterson (1996) reported that the women they studied had focused their lives around their husbands and his employment. It was through him that their status was determined and so without him they were at a loss until they had redefined themselves as women without husbands, from whom they could draw their identity. This was hardly the case for the majority of women in this study. Some middle-class women would have been happy to be identified through the high office of their husbands, but most of those widows had created a life of their own, in part separate from their husband while they were still married, and so were not known only through their husbands. These women had sources of power other than those with which they were associated as wives. Their husbands' passing would therefore not be so devastating. It would be a loss but hardly a deprivation of status and identity.

The issue of class proved to be important for the working-class women here, in that they were more likely to report that their lives had become harder, not exclusively because of widowhood, but because life is harder economically for the working class.

This chapter has shown us that many Jamaican widows are strong and independent, like the Jamaican women who are portrayed in Mathurin's (1975) *Rebel Woman*. Widowhood is stressful in many ways, and the widows in the study had to live with and within contradictory discourses that suggest, on one hand, that women "need a man" and will not do well without one, and, on the other, that older women should be caregivers for all their family. In all of this these Jamaican widows proved themselves to be tough and resilient. The majority did not treat widowhood as an occasion for self-pity and doubt but, after the initial shock, picked themselves up and resumed their normal course of doing what had to be done, not only for themselves but also for their families. This chapter has tried to help them to find a way of describing their experiences in their way, to construct a discourse in which contradictory feelings are allowed, and which allows us to acknowledge that marriage answers only some women's needs while others are met more adequately when women feel empowered because of their control of their time and money.

CONCLUSION

This study has weaved in and out of the lives of midlife and older women in two communities, one a working-class community (August Town) and the other a middle-class community (Hope Pastures). The research from which this book comes hypothesized that older women live within a framework of power that does not fully recognize their efforts and does not provide them with the necessary tools to do all that is expected of them by family and community. The research explored various aspects of the women's lives, with special attention being paid to their family life, and their interaction with various family members. The work women did in and outside the home, paid and unpaid, came under scrutiny and the importance of power in their various relationships was noted. Two other special areas of interest with regard to the hypothesis were women's health and the experience of widowhood.

With regard to the health of midlife and older women, the main concerns were the health status of the women who had been interviewed and whether or not the governmental health authorities saw them as a special group in need of health care. The research also sought to discover what the responses to their need for health care were, and what societal expectations existed with regard to their health. With regard to widowhood, the research sought to understand how this event changed women's lives and what part power played in women's responses to these changes.

The data showed that women of this age group were very important to their family and that their families were important to them. They were influenced by factors such as employment or unemployment, migration and their own health, as well as that of their relatives. What came across poignantly in this study was that despite all that these women did for their families, to provide income in their homes, and often providing the homes themselves, even family members who lived with the reality of these women's contributions, still did not see them as productive income earners, but primarily as caregivers. The familial discourse of women as caregivers denied the economic contribution they clearly made, and in so doing denied them both the status and the practical support that full acknowledgement of their dual contribution would have required.

Women of both groups, despite the class differences, had many similarities in relation to their family life. For example, in both groups, those who worked outside the home also had responsibilities within the home. And in both groups, some were aided in their domestic tasks by family members, who helped but preferred to be selective about the tasks with which they assisted.

Some of the working-class women of the August Town sample saw their children as a resource for the future. The middle-class women did not see their children that way. Although children were not seen as an investment for the future by middle-class women, almost equal percentages of women of both groups, 37 per cent for the working class and 42 per cent for the middle class, had adopted or fostered children. This means that both groups of women saw value in taking responsibility for children other than their own.

Within the Caribbean, one dominant societal expectation is that women of this age group will continue to "do" for children, even in their old age, and the data here showed that they did. But it was not always one-sided as there were at times reciprocal benefits. The interdependence involved house sharing, gifts, and health care on one another's behalf. The most outwardly manifest act of interdependence was that of house sharing. Thirty-one per cent of the working-class women and 55 per cent of the middle-class women had at least one adult offspring still in residence. House sharing in this situation took place in an environment in which rentals were especially high and mortgages astronomical. House sharing provided many reciprocal benefits for women and their families. Women had companionship and the children were able to save money, among other things. Although the interdependence through house sharing was not always beneficial to the women, they continued to share, with their daughters especially, because they hoped to grow emotionally closer to them and so have improved chances of care in their old age. The data showed that women of both groups were emotionally closest to their daughters.

Women of this age group, although presenting themselves as independent women, across both class groups were reluctant to make decisions without consulting family members, and only 5 per cent of the working-class women and 15 per cent of the middle class seemed sufficiently independent minded to go ahead with decisions with which their relatives had not agreed. This showed that, although these women seemed independent, and were often economic providers rather than provided for, they so cherished the relationship they had with relatives who were close, that they at times inconvenienced themselves rather than offend them.

With regard to their sexuality, women from midlife had to be especially cautious, particularly if they no longer resided with their spouses, or if they were widowed. There were a number of contradictions in the discourse concerning the sexuality of women of this age group and these women deliberately subdued aspects of their sexuality because of their fear of being in conflict with their grown offspring, church and wider society.

Large numbers of middle-class women, more than the working-class women, had relatives abroad. These included close relatives such as sons and daughters. One did not gain the impression that they saw this as a great advantage to themselves; they did not couch its significance in those terms, although it was clearly important. However, they were in contact with such relatives, and received occasional gifts and remittances from them.

Concern about the future was as important an issue for the women of Hope Pastures as it was for the women of August Town. The main concerns the middle-class women expressed were first loneliness, followed by economic security, a general concern for old age, and ill health. Those women need not have feared loneliness as much as they said they did, as the results of the research suggest a high degree of house sharing, especially with relatives. They might have expressed their fear of loneliness because some of them had not as yet faced the reality that they would not be on their own in their old age, especially if they owned their own home. With the economic crisis at the time not showing any sign of ending for the next several years, with the interest rate being as high as it was and with the difficulties young adults had acquiring residences for themselves, those women were not going to be lonely. The main concerns the working-class women expressed for the future were economic ones.

Women of this age group undoubtedly undertook many tasks in the society for family and community, yet in many ways they were taken for granted, and so had even more work piled on them. However, in the main, they responded positively to demands made on them by family and community. These demands ranged from minding children, with no financial assistance from those requesting such help, to sharing their homes, also without financial contribution. Many of the women, however, did these things because they felt that these acts would make life easier and better for their relatives, and also in so doing would improve their relationship with them. They did them, one could say, out of love.

The work these women did was very important to them, as well as to their families. Those who worked outside the home did so because they needed to, in order to maintain their relative independence and because the economic circumstances of their family and the declining value of any other income might have demanded this.

Women of this age group provided service to community members through a range of activities and through their involvement in community organizations. Here again they were still faithful to the tasks assigned to them, even when community members did not reimburse them for expenses incurred as they sought to provide service to the community. They aided the state by providing service for which the state would otherwise have had to take responsibility. Even in relation to their lives as widows, the women continued to make a contribution to family and society, by opening up their homes to be shared with adult offspring and other relatives.

One largely unrecognized contribution that women from midlife on made was in relation to the health of family and community members. The societal norm is that older women are assigned this responsibility and these roles are rarely ascribed to others. The denial of the economic contribution made by these women fed a belief, perhaps, that they had nothing much better to do. In relation to the underlying discourse, helping with people's health is really an extension of the caring role that family members assigned to midlife and older women.

One area of the life and health of the midlife and older woman that was not explored in the research for this book in 1990–91 was that of HIV/AIDS status. At the time of the research, the perception was that the disease was essentially a male homosexual problem. The disease was not new to the Caribbean, the first cases having been diagnosed as far back as 1982, but in terms of public perception the problem was essentially male. However, by the mid-1990s the epidemic was well underway. The public still perceived that men were at greater risk than women (Royes 1993). The implications for older persons, especially the older woman, would not have been uppermost in the minds of the community and researchers in the Caribbean. Since that time, the nature of the epidemic has changed and for the Caribbean, Jamaica included, there is now what is being referred to as the feminization of the HIV/AIDS epidemic (CAREC 2004).

By 2004, the face of the epidemic had changed completely and those most at risk for the disease were young women and girls (CAREC 2004), with serious implications for midlife and older women. In Jamaica, the epidemic was impacting on older women in a number of ways. Perhaps the most significant impact was that once more, those older women were being called upon to fulfil their caregiving roles. They had to provide care for their adult children and other family members who had been sickened by the virus. On the death of those younger relatives, the midlife and older women then needed to fill their most accustomed roles as caregivers to their grandchildren and other orphaned children. There was nothing new here: just an increase in the numbers. However, in the past, some of the parents of these children might have migrated and would then have provided some amount of financial support, some more reliably than others, to the older women who had been left in charge of their children. With the HIV/AIDS situation there was no such support, as the relatives had died.

Additionally, these grandparents – our midlife and older women – also have to cope with issues of stigma and discrimination because of their association with the HIV/AIDS epidemic. Undoubtedly the HIV/AIDS epidemic has added to the burdens that have traditionally been those of the midlife and older women.

By 2004, the antiretroviral drugs had become more available to persons living with HIV/AIDS in Jamaica, enabling a greater longevity for the infected. Some of these infected persons undoubtedly would have been women from the very age group examined in this book (Rawlins 2002b). More research is now required to determine the exact nature of the HIV/AIDs epidemic on the lives of midlife and older women.

Women of this age group were expected to be caregivers but there were situations in which they expressed their reluctance to undertake the expected caregiving roles, such as free childminding and chores for their daughters. Some then did what they thought at times was more important for themselves, given the realities of their daily existence. But this role rejection was not nearly as frequent as the converse.

This study has been something of an unveiling of the lives of Jamaican women aged fifty to seventy-four years. In the areas of their lives studied, we have observed the ways in which they have been influenced by the relationships they experienced with family members, community members and the existing social and economic situation of the country. Some of the findings, for example, that women of this age group make sacrifices for their adult offspring, even to their own disadvantage, were anticipated, as these understandings are in accord with the dominant discourses on older women.

However, what was much more interesting, and an unexpected finding, was evidence that women did not always accept the justice of these expectations, or feel the way they were discursively expected to feel. There were repressed discourses in every area of these women's lives; that is, discourses that were not commonly known, but which are shared only with others in their age group and inner circle of friends, or which were not fully formulated even at the time of the interviews. These discourses were important to the women's lives and influenced their daily interactions. The most important discourses that were revealed were in the areas of sexuality, where older women whose partners were alive continued to enjoy active sexual intimacies; health, where the women felt that their special needs as ageing women were not met; and widowhood, where the repressed and contradictory discourse of some portrayed men as expensive and widowhood as freedom, even while deeply mourning their loss.

It appears that with regard to this group of women, family and society have for generations clung steadfastly to a particular way of seeing them. In effect, the society has been experiencing what I would refer to as "discourse paralysis" in relation to such women, and consequently, no serious change has come about in relation to how these women are seen, nor has their contribution been fully recognized.

There is an urgent need for a shift in relation to society's view of this group of women. It is my hope that this book will contribute something towards this desired change by exposing the alternative discourses that women from midlife are already attempting to discuss.

The midlife and older women reported on here had concerns about their future; they were not pessimistic about it, nor were they overly optimistic. For example, they recognized that in relation to their health they were not treated as a special group, but hoped that in the future more would be done for them, as a group of "older women", and as a group with special health needs.

Jamaican society is currently experiencing a shift in the population structure, with older women representing a larger proportion. Undoubtedly such women will be called upon to fulfil even more roles, as we see with the HIV/AIDS epidemic. Consequently, more needs to be done for such women economically and socially, not only to enable them to perform these roles, but for their own satisfaction and health. As this group of women increases in size, as demographers predict it will, it is desirable that they should realize benefits such as improved opportunities for leisure, employment for those who want to be employed, and, most importantly, an improvement in their quality of life. It is hardly beneficial to these women to experience an improvement in their life expectancy if their lives are going to continue to be as stressful, or even more stressful, than it was in their more youthful days.

Improvements in the pensions and benefits available from the state would go a long way towards improving the quality of life of these women. Women complained that the state benefits were unrealistic given the increasing cost of living, and those who had not been in pensionable jobs or whose husbands had not been in jobs that contributed to the NIS, which administers the widow's benefits, were not eligible for these benefits. Such widows will need to lobby for a basic benefit for all widows in need and improved benefits for those who had contributed to the NIS. These additional benefits could be realized if funds collected by the NIS were invested creatively. Public education about the lives of older women and an easing of the housing situation for younger people would also improve the quality of life for these older women.

Midlife and older women have to lobby more persistently for themselves, for improvements in state benefits, for specialized health care, and for special employment programmes for those who desire or need re-employment after retirement.

Government policymakers also need to take note of the special situation surrounding the lives of some women from midlife. These policymakers should ensure that such women receive adequate pensions, health care and assistance in purchasing medical supplies and supplementary financial allowances in those situations where they undertake responsibilities for children, ageing family members, family members with HIV/AIDS and other community members.

NOTES

Introduction

1. See, for example, the calypsos reviewed by Rohlehr (1990). In one calypso, the older woman is presented negatively by the calypsonian, as someone who does not know when to quit sexually, and as someone who provides economic incentives to young men in return for sexual favours. She is ridiculed by the calypsonian as follows: "She is a widow by the name of Ma Christopher. Her younger son could be my father, but I don't mind . . . / The old lady is heaven your tea at eight and breakfast at eleven" (p. 234). Here we see the caregiving role maintained. She is also portrayed as an older insecure woman, who is emotionally dependent on the attention of young men, as we see in the calypsonian Ziegfield's song, "I Don't Want no Young Women": "You can do what you like, they don't get enraged / They 'fraid you might strike for a higher wage" (Rohlehr 1990, 233).

2. For an elaboration of the issues summarized here, see Rawlins (1996).

3. Working-class women are much less likely to be married or living in a home with a permanent partner than are middle-class women (Roberts and Sinclair 1978; Senior 1991). Although marriage is seen as an ideal in Jamaican society, it is still an institution about which working-class women think carefully before committing themselves. There is a history of late marriages in the Caribbean among this group, and these marriages sometimes take place after all the children are grown. One reason for the late marriage is that working-class women feel that they will lose their independence by marrying early.

4. At the end of 2000, the population fifty years and older was 445,800, with women representing 51.6 per cent (Planning Institute of Jamaica 2002).

5. Reference is being made here to women who had not been legally married, but who had been living in a common-law relationship with their partner or husband. I am using common-law relationship here as it is used in Jamaica to refer to those unions in

which the partners share a common residence but are not legally married (Roberts and Sinclair 1978). They are, in effect, also "widows", but having not been legally married, they are not termed widows.

6. This type of classification is possible in Jamaica, whereas it might not be possible in more developed societies, where people of different class groups live in the same community. The houses of the working class were usually wooden or made of bricks and were usually small (two or three rooms). If there were more than five rooms, quite often they would be in a state of incomplete and sometimes disordered construction. Education level was most often primary for the working class, and occupation was manual, service or lower-level clerical.

7. August Town had been home to a one-time spiritual leader named Alexander Bedward, an early millenarian whose teachings about a "worldly heaven and a heavenly world" are still remembered today. A small community named for him and still bearing his name was established in August Town. The members of that community have almost all died now, and the remaining ones would have been beyond the age of those being interviewed for this study (Post 1978).

8. In low-income communities such as August Town, it is not unknown for some people to connect their homes illegally to the Jamaica Public Service Company power supply; they are then able to receive electricity without having to pay for it.

9. Many urban working-class Jamaicans live in this yard-type situation. The yard is a complex in which several houses are situated. The houses are usually owned by one person, who rents the small houses, or rooms within larger houses, to individuals or families.

10. Marl is a type of soil found commonly in the mountains of Jamaica and is used in road-building.

11. The history of the establishment of the Social and Preventive Medicine Clinic is available within that institution. The clinic provides basic health services and more to the people of August Town, who speak very proudly of the clinic and the staff. It is open five days each week and provides antenatal and postnatal, paediatric, hypertensive and diabetic treatment as well as first aid to the people of the community. It also provides nutrition counselling and family planning services.

12. The original owners of the Hope Pastures houses were all "solid" middle-class persons, being professionals, business persons or top-level civil servants. Another characteristic of these early residents was that a significant number of them, maybe as many as 50 per cent of the original owners, were Jamaican whites, mixed-race persons and what in Jamaica are called "high brown", that is, persons of a light brown complexion, and a few persons of Chinese or Syrian origin. Most of them were Jamaicans by birth, which reflects the ethnic diversity of the island as it was then, but which has changed somewhat since 1962. The respondents stated that the population had changed. "Many of the whites, browns and Chinese had left in the 1970s, but there are many white and light-coloured people still living in the community, more so than could be found in the adjoining community of Mona

Heights," said one resident. In the absence of information on the racial composition of the population of Jamaica for 1962, the data from Carl Stone for 1972 and media reports for 1990 give us an indication of change. Carl Stone (1986, 3) gives the racial composition for Jamaica as follows: 78 per cent black, 15 per cent brown or light-skinned coloureds, 3 per cent Indians, 3 per cent whites and 1 per cent Chinese. The figures for 1990, which were fairly frequently quoted in the media, gave the racial breakdown for the population as 96 per cent African and Middle-Eastern or European extraction. The data, although not for Hope Pastures specifically, reflect the changing racial composition of the society as a whole, and concur with the trend described by the residents of Hope Pastures for their community.

13. By the year 2003, those houses were being sold for J$6 million to J$7 million.

14. I refer to this area as "upper" Hope Pastures as it was the second phase of the development as a residential area and it was on a slight elevation compared to the first.

15. The Statistical Package for Social Scientists® (SPSS) was used for data analysis.

16. The women from the case studies were chosen because their life situation was typical of the women in the group, and because they were a little more friendly and approachable than were the other women. To choose them I simply asked them if it would be possible for me to visit them repeatedly during the fieldwork period.

Chapter I

1. The population of Kingston and St Andrew was estimated at 565,000 in the year 2000 (Planning Institute of Jamaica 2000).

2. There had been no significant change by 2002, when the figure was 41.4 per cent (Planning Institute of Jamaica 2002).

3. Life expectancy in 2001 was 73.5 years for males and 77.6 years for females. (PAHO 2001).

4. The "mother country" was the term used to refer to the country that was the colonizing power.

5. Professor Headley's article was written with reference to a comment made by the government about the importance of remittances to the economy. The A and B accounts mentioned were special accounts that the government introduced to encourage Jamaican nationals living abroad, and others with access to foreign exchange, to invest their money in Jamaica. These accounts would be tax free, but would provide the country with foreign exchange that could be accessed by the state.

6. Alumina (aluminium oxide) is the product derived from bauxite ore. Aluminium is used as a valuable component in the aircraft industry and other industries.

7. "The rate of inflation accelerated towards the end of 1992, reaching an all time high of 80.2 percent for the year compared to 29.7 percent in 1990" (*Latin American Regional Report*, 2 April 1992, 1).

8. Jamaica indeed had an enviable record in health and educational services up to the mid-1970s, compared to many other developing countries, including other Caribbean

islands. Jamaica, as the largest English-speaking Caribbean island, was a favoured country under British colonial rule. That regime had laid down an infrastructure in health and education, which served not only Jamaica but also the smaller islands. The establishment of the University College of the West Indies, as the University of the West Indies was then called, with the first campus at Mona in Jamaica, also provided Jamaica with an advantage over other Caribbean islands, in that health and education personnel were trained locally and Jamaica reaped the benefits of such training earlier than the other islands.

9. That would have been approximately US$5 in 1990.

10. Contributions to the NIS are based on a two-tiered system; 2.5 per cent of the employee's gross salary matched by 2.5 per cent from the employer up to a maximum of J$15,080 in 1991. The contributions are paid by means of stamp-cards or deduction cards. Self-employed persons and voluntary contributors are responsible for their own stamp-cards and for ensuring that they keep them stamped and up to date. The NIS covers all persons who are gainfully occupied in insurable employment provided they are males between the ages of eighteen and seventy years or females between the ages of eighteen and sixty-five years. The insurable population is further placed in three categories, namely, employed persons, self-employed persons and voluntary contributors.

11. The widows in this study would not have been eligible for this allowance as it is really a spouse allowance paid to a male or female pensioner. The female pensioner may only receive this benefit if she has a dependent husband who is at least sixty years old, unable to work, and who has no income (Jamaica Information Service 1990, 6).

12. If contributors do not satisfy the contribution requirements for a pension, provided they have made fifty-two weekly contributions, they may receive a grant (Jamaica Information Service 1990, 6). It would be given in a lump sum, and would not be a large sum of money.

13. To receive a pension, however, one must meet certain conditions. In order to qualify for a pension one must have paid up to 312 contributions, a minimum yearly average of 13 contributions. A full flat-rate pension is payable if the yearly average falls below 39 contributions. Reduced rates are payable where the average falls below 39 (Jamaica Information Service 1990, 5).

Chapter 2

1. The works and the names of these authors will be familiar to social science students and researchers on the Caribbean and include Edith Clarke (1957), R.T. Smith (1956), M.G. Smith (1962) and Hermione McKenzie (1993).

2. Barrow (1988, 157) explains the approaches as follows: "The Cultural Diffusion approach attempts to explain family structure by referring to its roots in Africa, India and

Europe and argues that the present structures represent modifications of these origins."
The main proponent of the cultural diffusion approach was Herskovits (1941), whose thesis was that there persist until the present in Caribbean culture a number of elements of African culture. The social pathology approach claims that the hazards of the middle passage and plantation slavery have deformed the Afro-American family in a number of ways. The structural functionalist approach argues that the family is neither deformed nor dysfunctional, but has adopted certain forms as a response to a situation of poverty and economic marginality. Another approach to the family, which is less used, is the adaptive response approach, which incorporates some elements of functionalism. Adaptive response theorists, such as Gonzalez (1970) and Whitehead (1978), argue that families headed by women are not maladaptive, but are positive responses to the absence of males through migration. Gonzalez (1970) argues that the absence of a resident male in the family during peak periods of male unemployment is not disadvantageous to the household. The reasoning is that the absence of this potentially dominant and perhaps domineering figure enables the women of the family to maintain their social and economic linkages with female relatives and friends, unhindered by adult male advice and interference. Others of these theorists, notably Stoffle (1977) and Rubenstein (1983), argue that the movement from one union to another is an adaptive function, in response to the changing economic conditions of the region and the concomitant unpredictable economic status of their partners.

3. This type of unit is defined as female-headed even when there is a co-resident male partner.

4. Of the fifty persons interviewed on the specific perception question: "Number as 1 and 2 below the two words which are most likely to come to your mind when you think of women fifty years and over", 40 per cent said they thought of women from midlife as mothers first; 35 per cent said they saw women from midlife as grandmothers first and only 13 per cent saw them as workers first.

5. The question asked was: "Number in order of importance from one to nine what you see as the main roles which women from midlife play in Jamaican society."

6. That is, if the waged workers of the two communities are taken together.

7. Supporting evidence for this is found in the work of Roberts and Sinclair (1978) and McKenzie (1993).

8. With specific reference to current union status, the data showed the following for August Town and Hope Pastures, respectively: married, 29 per cent and 59 per cent; widowed, 17 per cent and 26 per cent; and single, 33 per cent and 8 per cent for the two communities. The differences are statistically significant, $p < .002$.

9. Some Caribbean researchers do not make a distinction between family and household. The data presented here for household is useful for discussions on family, in this context.

10. Eighty-one per cent of the working-class women who were in good health were expected to do the shopping, as were 75 per cent of the women of the middle class.

11. A "partner" is a rotating credit institution in which low-income persons each week pool a set sum of money. The entire amount, referred to as the "draw", is then given to one individual. In time each person will receive the entire sum collected for the week. This might also be done on a monthly basis and was more likely to be monthly where practised by middle-class women.

12. "Fadah" is the Jamaican patois word for father.

13. Juice frozen in a plastic bag.

14. The Common Entrance Examination was taken by primary school children at age eleven years, to secure a place within the secondary education system. If this examination was not passed, the child's educational opportunities could be negatively affected. The examination has since been abandoned and replaced by a system of continuous assessment referred to as the Sixth Grade Achievement Test.

15. To live alone in one's old age might appear to be the ideal if one is in good health, but the reality in Jamaica was that I did not meet one older person who wanted to live alone. Some, especially among the middle class, might have liked to have persons other than relatives living with them, for example, paying boarders, but the fear of burglars in the Kingston area meant that all women realized that life on one's own was not a luxury that they should crave.

16. With regard to home ownership, 39 per cent of the women from each community sample owned the home in which they lived. Some owned their home jointly with their spouse. This was the situation for 21 per cent of the August Town women and 32 per cent of the Hope Pastures women. For 6 per cent of the August Town women and 7 per cent of the Hope Pastures women, the house was owned by the spouse alone.

17. They would have negotiated with relatives to pay food and electricity bills, and in some instances minimal rents.

18. August Town women were concerned about a wide range of issues, for example, their economic security and what would happen to them generally as they grew older. These two factors were these women's main concerns. The other concerns that they had, in order of importance, were fear of ill health, unemployment, neglect by children and desertion by spouse. The differences in the concerns that the women of August Town and Hope Pastures mentioned were statistically significant and many women had not only one concern, but some had two, three and even four. However, what was similar for all of them was their concern about their economic security; this rated as the number one concern of the August Town women. The importance given to economic security by the two groups speaks to the women's understanding that for most of them their economic power decreased as they grew older and their problems were compounded by the national economic problems Jamaica faced in 1990–91. Women on small fixed incomes had witnessed the extremely serious erosion of their spending power and had good reason to worry about the future.

19. Her daughter, a divorcee, worked as a flight attendant and was frequently out of the country.

20. This was just barely the case, however, as middle-class women reportedly felt just as close to their husbands as to their mothers or sisters, while working-class women definitely felt closer to their daughters, then mothers or sisters, then sons, then husbands.

21. This would have been approximately US$200 in 1990 and US$40 in 2003, as a result of continuing devaluation of the dollar over the period.

22. A days worker is a person who sells her labour on a daily basis and might work for a number of different employers. The days worker makes more money at the end of the week if she works every day, because the daily rate is higher than it would be if the woman works a full week for one employer. Naturally the days worker does more physically by the end of the week than the employee who has one employer.

23. Not all the case studies have been included in the book. A total of twenty-five were done during the research period and sixteen have been included. The others are used for quotes and excerpts throughout the book.

24. It is not uncommon in Jamaica for several relatives to assist in providing the airfare for a relative to travel abroad. It is then expected that such relatives will provide financial assistance to those left behind in Jamaica once they have established themselves.

25. "Relative" here meant son, daughter, spouse, sister, brother or parent.

26. These barrels are literally that; they are filled with clothing and other gifts and shipped to Jamaica from relatives abroad.

27. The reference to "spare parts" here would relate to buying parts for cars and electrical appliances that are not readily available in Jamaica or where these items cost considerably more if they are purchased in Jamaica.

28. The difference in what the relatives abroad did was statistically significant by class.

29. Thirty-six per cent of the August Town women and 51 per cent of the Hope Pastures women stated that they did nothing for relatives abroad.

30. The category "illegitimate" was eliminated in Jamaica by law in 1976 through the Status of Children's Act.

31. Reference is made to this norm in the Caribbean literature. See, for example, C.L.R. James's *Minty Alley* (1981), where the middle-aged Mrs Rouse forgives her "spouse" time and again for his infidelity. Whatever was the true nature of these relationships, these women had come to terms with them and were "getting on with their lives" so to speak. Even if it meant ignoring their husband's extramarital relations, any such marital discord was not going to be used to unnecessarily overshadow or burden their daily existence.

32. They disclosed that of the total group of 170 who responded on this particular issue, seventy-seven were sexually active, meaning that they engaged in heterosexual intercourse.

33. Fifty-three per cent were middle class and 47 per cent were working class.

34. Once more it was the working-class group of women who showed themselves to be more conservative in their responses to the question, "What are your views on sex and women over fifty?" They expressed a greater concern for the woman's need to be married,

17.5 per cent compared with 6.7 per cent for the middle-class group. More of the middle-class women appeared to have an open view on women over fifty years old and sex, and a larger percentage, 37.1 compared to 5 per cent, stated that "intimate relations are ageless" and that "sex goes on as before", 14.6 per cent to 8.8 per cent for the working class. Generally speaking, the working-class women showed a greater concern for morality in their insistence that "sex is fine" as long as the women were married.

35. See, for example, the case of Mrs Gooden, Case no. 9 in chapter 3.

36. Women's roles changed from the time when they were very young to the time that they were close to age forty. Then it would seem that their roles, especially among working-class women, did not change very much between that time and the time that they reached the age of sixty years. When these women were young women, their mothers and grandmothers had done for them what they were now doing for their children and grandchildren. But having arrived in their late thirties and forties, they found that they had moved into the caring and the representative roles and that they usually had to serve many years in these capacities.

Chapter 3

1. One definition of the plural society is that used by M.G. Smith (1974, 9), who states that it is "the condition in which members of a common society are internally distinguished by fundamental differences in their institutional practices ... such differences ... normally cluster, and by their cluster they simultaneously identify institutionally distinct aggregates or groups, and establish deep social divisions between them".

2. Girls were disadvantaged particularly because of the patriarchal ideology but Miller (1986, 38) notes, "It seems safe to infer that less than 30 per cent of the black children were enrolled in the schools in 1871."

3. Miller cites Orlando Patterson's *The Sociology of Slavery* (1967, 113–44) as his source.

4. "Between 1834 and 1899, it appears that the majority of students recruited in the pupil teaching system were males" (Miller 1986, 17). Miller suggests that women were being actively discriminated against. He notes that after 1900 more women were employed as pupil teachers and enrolled in colleges for training as teachers.

5. Source: personal communication with older teachers in Jamaica 1991.

6. The unemployed in 1990–91 were recognized following the International Labour Organization's wider definition of unemployment. This broader perspective sees the unemployed not only as those persons seeking employment in the reference period (that is the week of the survey or six weeks prior to the census), but also those who did not look for a job, but wanted it and were available. This definition, therefore, includes those who are known as "job seekers" and the latter group "non job-seekers". Source: personal communication with Dr Patricia Anderson, demographer and senior lecturer, Department of Sociology and Social Work, University of the West Indies, Jamaica (October 1994). Incidentally, in the United States the latter category

of workers are referred to as "discouraged workers" and are not included when the unemployment rate is calculated.

7. In 2002, this proportion continued to increase and did so by 1.8 per cent over the previous year to 55.4 per cent of the labour force (Planning Institute of Jamaica 2002, section 21.3). In this survey, forty and fifty women of August Town and Hope Pastures, respectively, were employed full-time in waged employment. The middle-class women worked for government or for private companies, while the working-class women worked in service-type occupations or were self-employed. Although the retirement age is sixty years for women, outside of the governmental sector and the formalized private sector, the retirement age is not mandatory.

8. The population in 2003 was 2.63 million (Planning Institute of Jamaica 2003).

9. In 2002, female unemployment comprised 61.4 per cent of the unemployed labour force (Planning Institute of Jamaica 2003, chapter 21.6).

10. "Informal sector" here refers to that sector in Jamaica that is neither the government sector nor the organized private sector. The formal sector, as has been used here, is the government sector or the areas of employment within the organized private sector.

11. This was a relatively large sum of money for that type of activity in 1990–91.

12. The clothes and shoes were bought by an informal commercial importer (ICI), who paid her to sell the clothes.

13. The complete list of occupations for August Town was: cleaner, washerwoman, seamstress, teacher, domestic helper, chambermaid, hospital attendant, garment factory worker, coal seller, cook, farmer, nurse, shopkeeper, higgler, cashier, sales clerk, vendor, hairdresser, bus operator, housewife, factory worker, daycare attendant, shop assistant, office attendant, laundry worker and community health aide.

14. The complete list of occupations for Hope Pastures was: teacher, business woman, school principal, minister of religion, telephone operator, caterer, secretary, lecturer, director, training officer, accountant, librarian, social worker, housewife, assistant registrar, lawyer, real estate agent, nurse, nursing tutor, marketing manager, physician, executive director, health-care manager, supervisor, personnel manager, assistant editor, sales clerk, dress-designer, machine operator, cosmetologist, assistant administrator, academic social worker, welfare officer, credit officer, senior civil servant, insurance sales representative, factory worker, pharmacist and ledger clerk.

15. The average earnings per week of wages in all large establishments in the first three quarters of 1990 was J$386.86 (approximately US$48 in 1990–91). Large establishments were those that employed fifty or more persons on a full-time basis (Statistical Institute of Jamaica 1990a, 10).

16. In this survey the most frequently mentioned occupation was domestic service for the low-income women, and we note that the average wages for the domestic worker were approximately $200 per week in 1991. The salaries for government employees such as housekeepers and ward assistants were not much more, being

J$245.66 and J$267.88 per week. We note also that under structural adjustment, government-employed health workers who were housekeepers and ward assistants lost their jobs. Some of these women were the main income earners for their families. (Personal communication with Mrs C. Duncan, training officer, University Hospital of the West Indies.)

17. The Impact Programme provided employment for previously unemployed lower socio-economic groups during the People's National Party regime of 1972 to 1980.

18. Basic school is the term given in Jamaica to schools that provide preschool education to children prior to the age of six years, the official age for school entry. These schools are usually privately organized, but some are operated by the government.

19. Son no. 4, although unemployed, was supported by son no. 1.

20. The salary differences here were significantly different by class, $p < .002$.

21. It should be noted though that many of the August Town women worked in situations in which they were on their own, the sole employee. Therefore, they were not in a position to comment on discrimination towards older workers.

22. Isis Duarte reported on a pattern of large family size in the Dominican Republic, which reflected, not a neglect of family planning, but the combining of familial resources (cited in Deere 1990, 71).

23. The two daughters who returned home brought two children each. The two who had never left home had two each, thus there was a total of eight grandchildren.

24. The NIS pension was J$101 every other week. Her husband received a similar pension, which together gave them J$408 per month, which she said, "could be quite useful if only the two of us depended on it".

25. Private preparatory school fees in Kingston at the time ranged from J$1,000 to J$2,000 per three-month term.

Chapter 4

1. This information was intended to reflect the state of health of older persons around the time the research for this book was done.

2. Sennott-Miller (1989) reports this finding as puzzling, as no evidence of alcoholism or chronic hepatitis could be demonstrated that would have explained these conditions as major problems of older women.

3. The situation has not changed with regards to hypertension and diabetes, as we see in Gomez and Sealey (1997).

4. This fairly common practice in Jamaica, especially among lower-income households, was mentioned to me by various members of the nutrition team of the Caribbean Food and Nutrition Institute, Mona, Jamaica. I have also observed this practice over time in Jamaica and Mrs Dorothy Gregory, social worker of the Department of Social and Preventive Medicine, had also mentioned this practice to me many years ago in relation to children receiving inadequate protein in their diet.

5. Alleyne (2000) noted that approximately 50 per cent of Caribbean women remained anaemic for most of their lives.

6. With regard to the under-financing of the health sector, Le Franc (1990, 79) says, "Looking at the health sector in particular, Boyd (1988) calculated that in constant terms per capita, health expenditure fell by 33 per cent over the 1981–85 period, and the levels were below those of 1970s. There is not going to be much surprise about the consequences of these kinds of severe cut-backs on the public health delivery system."

7. It is interesting to note that the allocation for 2002 was 3 per cent (Planning Institute of Jamaica 2002).

8. Personal communication with Dr Denise Eldemire, Department of Social and Preventive Medicine, University of the West Indies, Jamaica, and Dr Eva Fuller, medical officer, Ministry of Health, Kingston, Jamaica.

9. We note that these assertions have to be viewed with some caution as they came from only one perspective, that is, the women themselves and not their relatives. But the consistency and the frequency of reference to this factor suggests that these women felt strongly about it.

10. Here the respondent was making reference to the negative images that were presented of the Kingston Public Hospital (KPH), in relation to the shortage of personnel and material resources in 1990–91. Levitt (1991, 52) notes, "Newspaper accounts of patients writhing in pain and bawling for help in the hopelessly understaffed outpatient department of Kingston Public Hospital make sickening reading."

11. What happened with Mrs Steadman would not have been expected if she had not been married. In the situation of the common-law relationship, the "husband" would perhaps not have returned home, and if he did, the "wife" would not be obliged to accommodate him.

12. The differences were statistically significant, $p < .0111$.

13. The difference here by age for those who suffered no illness at all was statistically significant, $p < .0218$.

14. The explanation I have for the difference is that the middle-class women tended to work more in formal situations, and were not able to cope with the practical distractions that the problems of fibroids present. The working-class women worked in less formal situations, and were able to reorganize their workday, or cope with the practical inconveniences associated with this problem, because they were in domestic-type situations. Consequently they were able to cope with the side effects of uterine fibroids until they reached the natural menopause, and did not have to undergo surgery.

15. Six weeks is the period of time most women who have hysterectomies are told by their surgeons that they will need to get back to "normal" function.

16. See chapter 1, note 10. Possessing NIS stamp-cards ensures that the insured person qualifies for the available benefit.

17. Reference is made to this restructuring of the health sector in chapter 3.

18. The sick role is a particular type of behaviour that an individual who is sick, usually for more than a short period of time, might adopt. This term was introduced by Parsons (1951), who argued that the sick role legitimizes the deviant behaviour caused by the illness. The sick person knows that through society's acceptance of this role, he or she can expect to be exempted from some normal social activities and in some instances might take advantage of this social acceptance.

Chapter 5

1. In all Western countries, for every age group, starting at birth, the mortality is greater for males than it is for females.

2. An update on life expectancy for women in Jamaica in 2003 shows it as seventy-seven years for women and seventy-three years for men (PAHO 2003).

3. The 1982 Census of Jamaica shows that in the age group fifteen to forty-four years, almost equal numbers of women are in common-law relationships as are married, being 100,015 common-law and 156,950 married. The relevance here is that although large numbers of women are in common-law relationships in their earlier years, this is not the case in later years, and is one reason why there are many common-law wives, but few common-law widows. In this study, for example, there were no such women. Women tend to move out of these relationships in their forties, if the men will not marry them. Consequently, when these men die, they would not have been living with these particular women, who therefore would not consider themselves as widows.

4. The fifty women had been legally married.

5. Loneliness was the response for five women of August Town and fourteen women of Hope Pastures.

6. "Financial difficulties" was the response given by a total of six women, five of whom were from August Town.

7. Those in the sample had been widowed for an average of twelve years for the August Town sample and nine years for the Hope Pastures sample.

8. To "eat someone down" is a local Jamaican expression, which means to misuse or abuse someone's financial resources.

9. The different reasons that the women of the two communities gave were statistically significant, $p < .0040$.

10. An old-age grant is J$360.00 for the first fifty-two flat-rate contributions paid; J$7.20 for each additional thirteen flat-rate contributions paid; and J$9.36 for every unit of J$13.00 paid by the insured person, as well as age-related contributions (Jamaica Information Service 1990, 6). The reference to wage-related contributions is to the fact that in addition to flat-rate contributions, persons earning J$12.00 per week and over are required to pay wage-related contributions on wages between J$12.00 and J$290.00 at the rate of $0.10 per J$2.00, and contributed jointly by employer and employee, each paying $0.05.

11. The conditions in 1990–91 were that the deceased husband must either have paid a minimum of 312 weekly contributions, with an annual average of thirty-nine contributions and over, and reduced rates where the annual average falls between thirteen and thirty-nine contributions. The widow must also satisfy at least one of the following conditions at the date of her husband's or partner's death: (1) She must be married to her late husband, or have been living with her late partner in a common-law union for at least three years, and she must be fifty-five years old or over; be pregnant by her late husband or partner; (2) be married for at least three years and be permanently incapable of work because of a specified disease or mental or physical disablement; (4) be caring for a child of their family, who is less than eighteen years old. If the widow satisfies none of these conditions, but was married for at least three years she may receive pension for one year (Jamaica Information Service 1990, 7–8).

12. In 1990–91, Mrs Sybil Francis, president of the Council for the Aged and spokesperson on ageing in Jamaica faulted the government for not adjusting the pension system for the past twenty years, resulting in those who had retired in 1970 living at or below the poverty line in 1990.

REFERENCES

Alleyne, G. 2000. "Women's Health and the Double Burden". Presented as the Dr Elizabeth Quamina Memorial Lecture, Port of Spain, Trinidad, 3 October 2000.

Anderson, Patricia. 1989. *Levels of Poverty and Household Food Consumption in Jamaica*. Kingston: Institute of Social and Economic Research, University of the West Indies.

Antrobus, Peggy. 1987. "The Impact of the Debt Crisis on Jamaican Women". Paper presented at the First Meeting of Caribbean Economists, Kingston, Jamaica, University of the West Indies.

———. 1989. "The Impact of the Structural Adjustment Policies on Women". *CAFRA News* (September–November): 7–11.

Bankoff, E.A. 1983. "Social Support and Adaptation to Widowhood." *Journal of Marriage and the Family* 45, no. 4: 827–39.

Barrett, M. 1980. *Women's Oppression Today: Problems in Marxist Feminist Analysis*. London: Verso.

Barrow, C. 1988. "Anthropology: The Family and Women". In *Gender in Caribbean Development*, edited by P. Mohammed and C. Shepherd. Port of Spain, Trinidad: HEM Press.

Blenkner, M. 1965. "Social Work and Family Relations in Later Life with Some Thoughts on Filial Maturity". In *Social Structure and the Family Generational Relations*, edited by G. Streib and E. Shanas. Englewood Cliffs, NJ: Prentice Hall.

Boyd, D. 1988. *Economic Management, Income Distribution and Poverty in Jamaica*. New York: Praeger.

Burke, G.Y. 1983. *The Health of Caribbean Women in Midlife: Concerning Women and Development*. Barbados: Extra Mural Department, University of the West Indies.

Burkhauser, R.K., C. Holden and D.A. Myers. 1986. "Marital Disruption and Poverty: The Role of Survey Procedures in Artificially Creating Poverty". *Demography* 23: 621–33.

Byles, J.E., S. Feldman and G. Mishra. 1999. "For Richer for Poorer, in Sickness and in Health: Older Widowed Women's Health, Relationship and Financial Security". *Women's Health* 29, no. 1: 15–30.

Caribbean Epidemiology Centre (CAREC). 2004. *Status and Trends Analysis: Analysis of the Caribbean HIV/AIDS Epidemic 1982–2002*. Port of Spain, Trinidad: CAREC/PAHO/WHO.

Carr, D., K.S. House, C. Wortman, R. Nesse and R.C. Kessler. 2001. "Psychological Adjustment to Sudden and Anticipated Spousal Loss among Older Widowed Persons". *Gerontological Bulletin of Psychological Sciences and Social Sciences* 56, no. 4: S237–48.

Clarke, Edith. 1957. *My Mother Who Fathered Me: A Study of the Families in Three Selected Communities of Jamaica*. London: Allen and Unwin.

Cornia, G.A., R. Jolly and F. Stewart, eds. 1987. *Adjustment with a Human Face: Protecting the Vulnerable and Promoting Growth*. Oxford: Clarendon Press.

Cumper, G., W. Walker and C. McCormack. 1985. "Evaluation of Health Care in Jamaica". Mimeo. Kingston: Ministry of Health.

Davies, O., and Patricia Anderson. 1987. "The Impact of the Recession and Adjustment Policies on Poor Urban Women in Jamaica". Paper prepared for the United Nations Children's Fund, Kingston, Jamaica, September.

Deere, Carmen D. 1990. *In the Shadows of the Sun: Caribbean Development Alternatives and US Policy*. Boulder: Westview Press.

Department of Statistics. 1982. *Demographic Statistics of Jamaica*. Kingston: Department of Statistics.

Dirks, R., and V. Kerns. 1976. "Mating Patterns and Adaptive Change in Rum Bay 1823–1970." *Social and Economic Studies* 25, no. 1: 24–35.

Dressler, W. 1992. "Social Factors Mediating Social Class Differences in Blood Pressure in a Jamaican Community". *Social Science and Medicine* 35, no. 10: 1233–44.

Durant-Gonzalez, V. 1980. "Role and Status of Rural Jamaican Women: Higglering and Mothering". PhD dissertation, University of California.

Economic Commission on Latin America and the Caribbean (ECLAC). 1984. *Economic Survey of Latin America and the Caribbean*. Port of Spain, Trinidad: ECLAC.

Eldemire, Denise. 1989. "Medical Care for the Elderly: A Study in Kingston Jamaica". In *Midlife and Older Women in Latin America and the Caribbean*. Washington, DC: Pan American Health Organization and the American Association of Retired Persons.

———. 1993. "An Epidemiological Survey of the Elderly in Jamaica". PhD thesis, University of the West Indies, Jamaica.

———. 2002. "The Contribution of Seniors to Development: Family and Community". Paper prepared for the WHO/PAHO Collaborating Centre on Ageing, Department of Community Health and Psychiatry, University of the West Indies, Jamaica.

Farkas, J., and C. Himes. 1997. "The Influence of Caregiving and Employment on

Voluntary Activities of Midlife and Older Women". *Journal of Gerontology: Social Sciences* 52B, no. 4: S180–89.

Foucault, Michel. 1971. *The History of Sexuality*. New York: Pantheon Books.

Girvan, Norman, R. Bernal and W. Hughes. 1980. "The IMF and the Third World: The Case of Jamaica (1974–1980)". *Development Dialogue*, no. 2: 113–55.

Glaser, K., and C. Tomassini. 2000. "Proximity of Older Women to Their Children: A Comparison of Britain and Italy". *Gerontologist* 40, no. 6: 729–37.

Gomez, E., and K. Sealey. 1997. "Women, Health and Development". In *Health Conditions in the Caribbean*. Pan American Health Organization Scientific Publication, no. 561, 131–57. Washington, DC: PAHO.

Gonzalez, N.L. 1970. "Towards a Definition of Matrifocality". In *Afro American Anthropology: Contemporary Perspectives*, edited by Norman E. Whitten, Jr. and J.F. Szwed, 231–44. New York: Free Press.

Gordon, D. 1987. *Class, Status and Social Mobility in Jamaica*. Kingston: Institute of Social and Economic Research, University of the West Indies.

Graham, H. 1982. "Coping, or How Mothers Are Seen and Not Heard". In *On Problems of Men*, edited by S. Frudmarsh and E. Sarah. London: The Women's Press.

Grell, G., ed. 1987. *The Elderly in the Caribbean*. Proceedings of a Continuing Medical Education Conference. Kingston: University of the West Indies.

Henriques, F. 1953. *Family and Colour in Jamaica*. London: Eyre and Spottiswood.

Herskovits, M.J. 1941. *The Myth of the Negro Past*. Boston: Beacon.

Horowitz, A. 1982. "Adult Children as Care Givers to Elderly Parents: Correlates and Consequences". PhD dissertation, Columbia University.

Hyman, H.H. 1983. *Of Time and Widowhood*. Durham, NC: Duke University Press.

Jamaica Bureau of Women's Affairs. 1982. *Jamaica National Policy Statement on Women*. Kingston: Jamaica Bureau of Women's Affairs.

Jamaica Information Service. 1990. *All About National Insurance*. Kingston: Jamaica Information Service.

James, C.L.R. 1981. *Minty Alley*. London: New Beacon.

Johnson, M. 1986. "Domestic Service in Jamaica (1920–1970)". Paper presented at a Symposium on Caribbean Economic History, University of the West Indies, Kingston, Jamaica, 7–8 November.

Kanachi, L.S., P.S. Jones and P.E. Galbraith. 1996. "Social Support and Depression in Widows and Widowers". *Journal of Gerontological Nursing* 22, no. 20: 39–45.

Le Franc, E. 1990. "Socio-economic Aspects of Health: The Caribbean Region". In Proceedings of the Inaugural Meeting and Conference of the Caribbean Public Health Association (CARIPHA), Kingston, Jamaica, 24–26 October 1988.

Levitt, Kari. 1991. *The Origins and Consequences of Jamaica's Debt Crisis 1970–1990*. Kingston: Consortium Graduate School of Social Sciences, University of the West Indies.

Lobell, R.A. 1986. "Women in the Jamaica Labour Force 1881–1921". Paper presented at the Symposium on Caribbean Economic History, University of the West Indies, Kingston, Jamaica, 7–9 November.

Lopata, H.Z. 1973. *Widowhood in an American City*. Cambridge, Mass.: Schenckman.

———. 1979. *Women as Widows: Support Systems*. New York: Elsevier.

———. 1986. *Dissolution through Widowhood*. Chicago: Loyola University Press.

Louet, F., M. Grosh and J. Van der Gaag. 1993. *Welfare Implications of Female Headship in Jamaican Households*. Washington, DC: World Bank.

Massiah, Joycelin. 1982. "Female Headed Households in the Caribbean". *Women's Studies International* (July).

———. 1983. *Women as Heads of Households in the Caribbean: Family Structure and Feminine Status*. London: UNESCO.

Mathurin, Lucille. 1975. *Rebel Woman in the British West Indies*. Kingston: Institute of Jamaica.

McKenzie, Hermione. 1993. "The Family, Class and Ethnicity in the Future of the Caribbean". In *Race, Class and Gender in the Future of the Caribbean*, edited by J.E. Greene. Kingston: Institute of Social and Economic Research, University of the West Indies.

Miller, Errol. 1986. *The Marginality of the Black Male*. Kingston: Institute of Social and Economic Research, University of the West Indies.

Mohammed, Patricia, and Althea Perkins. 1999. *Caribbean Women at the Crossroads*. Kingston: Canoe Press.

Momsen, Janet. 1989. "Women and the Life Cycle in the Rural Caribbean". Paper presented at the annual meeting of the Society for Caribbean Studies, Hoddesdon, Hertfordshire.

———. 1993. *Women and Change in the Caribbean: A Pan-Caribbean Perspective*. Kingston: Ian Randle Publishers.

Morgan, L.A. 1981. "Economic Change at Mid-Life". *Journal of Marriage and the Family* 43: 899–912.

Morrison, Errol, I. Haye, Kushan Amarakoon, Fay Whitbourne, Judith Kirlew and Charles R. van West. 2001. "An Interim Report of an Intervention Strategy for Diabetes Care in Jamaica". *West Indian Medical Journal* 50, suppl. 1 (1–4 March): 55–59.

Murdock, M.E., C.A. Guarnaccia, B. Hayslip Jr. and C.L. McKibbin. 1998. "The Contribution of Small Events to the Psychological Distress of Married and Widowed Older Women". *Journal Women Aging* 10, no. 20: 3–22.

Pan American Health Organization (PAHO). 1985. *Health of Women in the Americas*. PAHO Scientific Publication, no. 488. Washington, DC: PAHO.

———. 2001. *Health Situation in the Americas: Basic Indicators*. Washington, DC: PAHO.

———. 2003. *Health Situation in the Americas: Basic Indicators*. Washington, DC: PAHO.

Parsons, Talcott. 1951. *The Social System*. New York: Free Press.

Patterson, I. 1996. "Participation in Leisure Activities by Older Adults after a Stressful Life Event: The Loss of a Spouse". *International Journal of Aging and Human Development* 42, no. 2: 124–42.

Patterson, Orlando. 1967. *The Sociology of Slavery: An Analysis of the Origins, Development and Structure of Negro Society in Jamaica.* London: MacGibbon and Kee.

Phillipson, C. 1980. "Women in Later Life: Patterns of Control and Subordination". In *Controlling Women,* edited by B. Hutter and G. Williams. London: Croom Helm

Planning Institute of Jamaica. 1985. *Economic and Social Surveys of Jamaica.* Kingston: Planning Institute of Jamaica.

———. 1990. *Economic and Social Surveys of Jamaica.* Kingston: Planning Institute of Jamaica.

———. 2000. *Economic and Social Surveys of Jamaica.* Kingston: Planning Institute of Jamaica.

———. 2002. *Economic and Social Surveys of Jamaica.* Kingston: Planning Institute of Jamaica.

———. 2003. *Economic and Social Surveys of Jamaica.* Kingston: Planning Institute of Jamaica.

Popay, Jenny. 1992. "My Health Is All Right, but I'm Tired All the Time: Women's Experience of Ill Health". In *Women's Health Matters,* edited by Helen Roberts. London: Routledge.

Post, Ken. 1978. *Arise Ye Starvelings: The Jamaica Labour Rebellion and its Aftermath.* The Hague: Martinus Nijoff.

Powell, Dora. 1984. "The Role of Women in the Caribbean". *Social and Economic Studies* 33, no. 2: 97–122.

Ramazanoglu, C., ed. 1993. *Up Against Foucault.* London: Routledge.

Rawlins, Joan M. 1988. "Life Cycle Events and the Work of Women in Two Urban Jamaican Communities". Unpublished paper, Institute of Social and Economic Research, University of the West Indies, Jamaica.

———. 1989a. "Widowhood in Jamaica: A Neglected Aspect of the Family Life Cycle". *Journal of Comparative Family Studies* 20, no. 3: 327–39.

———.1989b. "Widowhood: The Social and Economic Consequences in the Caribbean". In *Midlife and Older Women in Latin America and the Caribbean,* Washington, DC: Pan American Health Organization and the American Association for Retired Persons.

———. 1996. "Women from Midlife: Coping in Jamaica". PhD thesis, Institute of Social Studies, The Hague.

———. 2001. "Caring for the Chronically Ill Elderly in Trinidad". *West Indian Medical Journal* 50, no. 2: 13–16.

———. 2002a. "Daughters and Wives as Informal Caregivers of the Chronically Ill Elderly". *Journal of Comparative Family Studies* 33: 125–37.

———. 2002b. "HIV/AIDS and the Older Person in the Caribbean: A Preview". Paper presented at the twenty-seventh annual Caribbean Studies Association Conference, Nassau Beach Hotel, Nassau, Bahamas, 26 May–1 June.

Rawlins, Joan M., and Carolyn Sargent. 1989. *Factors Influencing Antenatal Health Care Among Low Income Jamaican Women.* Final project document presented to the International Center for Research on Women, Washington, DC.

Roberts, G.W., and S. Sinclair. 1978. *Women in Jamaica.* Milwood, NY: K.T.O. Press.

Rodman, Hyman. 1978. "Marital Careers in Trinidad". *Journal of Marriage and the Family* 40, no. 1: 156–63.

Rohlehr, Gordon. 1990. *Calypso and Society in Pre-Independence Trinidad.* Tunapuna, Trinidad: Gordon Rohlehr

Royes, Heather. 1993. *Jamaican Men and Same Sex Activities: Implications for HIV/STD Prevention.* Washington, DC: Academy for Educational Development, AIDSCOM.

Rubenstein, H. 1983. "Caribbean Household Organization: Some Conceptual Clarifications". *Journal of Comparative Family Studies* 14, no. 3: 283–98.

Sanchez, D. 1989. "Informal Supports Systems of Widows over 60 in Puerto Rico". In *Midlife and Older Women in Latin America and the Caribbean.* Washington, DC: Pan American Health Organization and the American Association for Retired Persons.

Sargent, Carolyn, and Joan Rawlins. 1991. "Factors Influencing Antenatal Health Care Among Low Income Jamaican Women". *Human Organization* 50, no. 2: 179–87.

Schlesinger, B. 1980. "Widows and Widowers in New Zealand". *Journal of Comparative Family Studies* 11, no. 1: 49–56.

Senior, Olive. 1991. *Working Miracles.* London: James Currey.

Sennott-Miller, L. 1989. "The Health and Socio-Economic Situation of Mid-Life and Older Women in Latin America and the Caribbean". In *Midlife and Older Women in Latin America and the Caribbean.* Washington, DC: Pan American Health Organization and the American Association for Retired Persons.

Simey, T.S. 1946. *Welfare and Planning in the West Indies.* London: Clarendon Press.

Singh, Harry. 2002. "Health Risk Behaviour in Women in Urban and Rural Trinidad". Paper presented in Seminar Series, Public Health and Primary Care Unit, Faculty of Medical Sciences, University of the West Indies, Trinidad and Tobago.

Smith, M.G. 1962. *West Indian Family Structure.* Seattle: University of Washington Press.

———. 1974. *The Plural Society in the British West Indies.* Kingston: Sangster's Book Stores.

Smith, R.T. 1956. *The Negro Family in British Guiana.* London: Routledge and Kegan Paul.

———. 1982. "Family, Social Change and Social Policy in the West Indies". *Nieuve West Indische Gids* 56, nos. 3–4: 260–72.

Standing, Guy. 1981. *Unemployment and Female Labour in Jamaica.* London: Macmillan.

Statistical Institute of Jamaica. 1982. *Census of Jamaica.* Kingston: Statistical Institute of Jamaica.

———. 1989. *Jamaica Survey of Living Conditions.* Kingston: Statistical Institute of Jamaica.

———. 1990a. *Employment, Earnings and Hours Worked in Large Establishments (1989–1990).* Kingston: Statistical Institute of Jamaica.

———. 1990b. *Labour Force Survey.* Kingston: Statistical Institute of Jamaica.

Stevens, C. 1983. "Alternatives for Financing the Demand for Health Service in Jamaica". Mimeo. Mona, Jamaica: Department of Social and Preventive Medicine, University of the West Indies.

Stoffle, R.W. 1977. "Industrial Impact on Family Formation in Barbados, West Indies". *Ethnology* 16, no. 3: 3–4.

Stone, Carl. 1986. *Class, State and Democracy in Jamaica.* New York: Praeger.

Townshend, P. 1965. "The Effects of Family Structure on the Likelihood of Admission to an Institution in Old Age". In *Social Structure and the Family Generational Relations*, edited by G. Streib and E. Shanas. Englewood Cliffs, NJ: Prentice Hall.

United Nations Children's Fund (UNICEF)/Planning Institute of Jamaica. 1991. *Situational Analysis of the Status of Children and Women in Jamaica*. Kingston: UNICEF/ Planning Institute of Jamaica.

United Nations (UN). 1992. *Aging Health and Disability*. DP1/1253, August, 1992-6M. New York: UN Department of Information.

Utz, R.L., D. Carr, R. Nesse and C.B. Wortman. 2002. "The Effects of Widowhood on Older Adults' Social Participation: An Evaluation of Activity, Disengagement, and Continuity Theories". *Gerontologist* 42, no. 4: 522–33.

Waldron, I., M. Nowotarski and M. Freimer. 1982. "Cross Cultural Variation in Blood Pressure". *Social Science and Medicine* 16: 419–30.

Wells, Y.D., and H.L. Kendig. 1997. "Health and the Well-Being of Spouse Caregivers and the Widowed". *Gerontologist* 37, no. 5: 666–74.

Whitbourne, Fay. 1999. "Diabetes in the Peri-Menopausal Period". *West Indian Medical Journal* 48, suppl. 1 (7 March): 14.

Whitehead, T.L. 1978. "Kinship and Mating as Survival Strategies: A West Indian Example". *Journal of Marriage and the Family* 40, no. 4: 817–28.

Wilson, Desiree. 1992. "Health and Sexuality of a Group of Mature Female Employees of the Staff of the University of the West Indies". Paper presented at a Women and Development Studies/Faculty of Medical Sciences Seminar, Barbados, 12 October.

Zick, C.D., and K. Smith. 1986. "Intermediate and Delayed Effects of Widowhood on Poverty". *Gerontology* 26: 669–75.

———. 1988. "Recent Marriage and Changes in Economic Well-Being". *Journal of Marriage and the Family* 50, no. 1: 233–44.

INDEX

household chores, 142; widowhood and, 125–126
housing: structural adjustment programmes and, 27
husbands. *See* spouses
hypertension, 93, 98–99, 100, 101, 103–104
hysterectomies, 103

illness: women's perception of, 99–100, 101, 103, 112. *See also* health
income. *See* wages
income earning, 142; in retirement, 86–88, 88–89, 92
inflation: and structural adjustment programmes, 28
isolation: widowhood and, 8. *See also* loneliness
International Monetary Fund (IMF): structural adjustment programmes, 25–26

Jamaica: geographic description, 24
Jamaica Bureau of Women's Affairs, 2
Jamaican family, 35
James, C.L.R.: and sexuality of older women, 119
job satisfaction, 83–84

labour: gendered division of, 7, 88
labour force: female participation in the, 72–74
labour shortage: 29
liberation: widowhood and, 118–119, 122–130
Lindo, Mrs: case study no. 16 (Hope Pastures), 129–130
liver disease, 93
loneliness: widowhood and, 5, 120, 129, 131, 139, 143. *See also* isolation

male/female relationships: midlife/older women and, 62
"manless woman": widowhood and the, 129–130
Manley government (1970s): and IMF policies, 26
manufacturing: women employed in, 72
marriage: women and, 37
matrifocal: defining, 35
medication: cost of, 103
men: social activities of, 42
menorrahgia, 105
middle-class women: and marriage, 37; relationship with adult children, 43–53; with partners, 38–41, 67; and sexuality, 64
midlife/older women, defining, 2
migration: and the economy, 33; and families, 9; to the US, 25
Miller, Errol: and education for boys, 70
Miller, Mrs: case study no. 8 (Hope Pastures), 82–83
Ministry of Health: expenditure, 96
mortality rates: causes of, 92; declining, 24; gender and, 117
mother/daughter relationships, 44–45
mother/son relationships, 45, 63
motherhood, 35–36
movement: widowhood and freedom of, 128

National Family Planning Board, 24
National Insurance Scheme (NIS): benefits, 29–31; for widows, 136–138, 147
Neil, Mrs: case study no. 14 (Hope Pastures), 124–125
non-remunerated work, 84–86
Norma: case study no. 4 (August Town), 58–59
nuclear family: defining the, 34
nurses: shortage of, 29